Pillsbury Best Muffins and Quick Breads

COOKBOOK

Pillsbury Best Muffins and Quick Breads

COOKBOOK

Favorite Recipes from
America's Most-Trusted Kitchens

The Pillsbury Company

Clarkson Potter/Publishers
New York

Credits

Pillsbury Publications
The Pillsbury Company

Publisher: Sally Peters
Publication Manager: Diane B. Anderson
Senior Editor: Maureen Rosener
Senior Food Editor: Andrea Bidwell
Recipe Editor: Nancy Lilleberg
Contributing Writers: Mary Caldwell, Kitty Shea
Photography: Graham Brown Photography, Tad
    Ware Photography
Food Stylists: Sue Brosious, Sue Brue, JoAnn Cherry,
    Sue Finley, Sharon Harding, Cindy Ojczyk,
    Lisa Golden Schroeder, Barb Standal
Recipe Typists: Michelle Barringer, Jackie Ranney

Pillsbury Publications

Publisher: Sally Peters
Publication Managers: Diane B. Anderson,
    William Monn
Senior Editors: Maureen Rosener, Jackie Sheehan
Senior Food Editor: Andi Bidwell
Test Kitchen Coordinator: Jill Crum
Circulation Manager: Karen Goodsell
Circulation Coordinator: Rebecca Bogema
Recipe Typists: Bev Gustafson, Mary Prokott,
    Nolan Vaughan

Bake-Off® is a registered trademark of
    The Pillsbury Company.
Bundt® is a registered trademark of Northland
    Aluminum Company

Published by Clarkson Potter/Publishers, 201 East 50th
Street, New York, New York 10022. Member of the Crown
Publishing Group.

Random House, Inc. New York, Toronto, London,
Sydney, Auckland
www.randomhouse.com

CLARKSON N. POTTER, POTTER, and colophon are trade-
marks of Clarkson N. Potter, Inc.

Printed in Japan

Design by Julie Baker Schroeder

Library of Congress Cataloging-in-Publication Data
Pillsbury, best muffins and quick breads: favorite recipes from
America's most-trusted kitchens / The Pillsbury Company. —
1st ed.
Includes index.
1. Muffins. 2. Bread. I. Pillsbury Company.
TX770.M83P55   1999
641.8'15—dc21   98-38176
                                                 CIP

ISBN 0-609-60283-7

10 9 8 7 6 5 4 3 2 1

First Edition

641.8
15
Pill

Clarkson Potter/Publishers

The Crown Publishing Group

President and Publisher: Chip Gibson
Vice President–Editorial Director: Lauren
    Shakely
Senior Editor: Katie Workman
Editorial Assistant: Julia Coblentz
Designer: Julie Baker Schroeder
Executive Managing Editor: Laurie Stark
Managing Editor: Amy Boorstein
Senior Production Manager: Jane Searle
Publicist: Wendy Schuman

Previous page: Apple Streusel Coffee Cake, page 200

Frontispiece: Zucchini-Orange Bread, page 165

Contents

Raspberry-Lemon Muffins with Streusel Topping, page 36

Cherry-Pistachio Scones, page 36

Brown Bread, page 192

Blueberry-Poppy Seed Brunch Cake, page 202

Muffins and Quick Breads Know-How

Muffins and quick breads hold their very own magic. The basics—flour, sweetener, butter or oil, egg—take on wonderfully varied character depending on what you choose for flavorings and "extra" ingredients such as fruit or nuts. These quick-fix breads are very gratifying for beginning and expert bakers alike, as the preparation and baking are quick and the results, superb. Whether you need a hearty muffin to start the day, an elegant loaf to slice for a brunch celebration or even a savory specialty to accompany lunch or supper, you'll find the right recipe in this book.

We've divided this book into chapters devoted to Sweet Muffins; Savory Muffins; Biscuits, Scones, Popovers and Doughnuts; Quick Breads; Coffee Cakes; and Butters and Spreads. Below, we've outlined information common to all the chapters.

Basic Ingredients

The quality of your ingredients has a definite effect on the flavor and quality of your finished baked goods. While muffins and quick breads may be embellished with cheese, nuts, candy, fruit, herbs and spices, they depend on a basic core of ingredients, including:

Flour

Most of the recipes in this book specify all-purpose flour and have been tested in our kitchens as such. Use either bleached or unbleached. Do not substitute bread flour, which has a higher gluten content that can result in tough muffins.

Most basic muffin or quick bread recipes also yield good results made with half whole wheat flour. Made entirely with whole wheat flour, however, they won't rise quite as high and their texture will be more dense.

To measure flour, spoon it into a dry measuring cup, then level off the top with the flat side of a knife. Don't measure by scooping the cup into the flour bin; this invariably results in too much flour going into the recipe, which makes the final result dry and crumbly.

Butter, Margarine, and Oil

Butter or another fat provides tenderness and moisture. Butter offers more flavor, but the recipes in this book yield excellent results when made with either regular butter or regular margarine, unless only one is specified. If the butter is to be creamed, set it out at room temperature for about an hour to soften. You can speed this process in the microwave so long as you watch it carefully—it takes only seconds to go from soft to liquid.

Whipped margarines or butters have been processed with air to yield a lighter-textured, easier-to-spread topping. They're not ideal for baking, but if they're all you have available, use them by weight rather than volume; 8 ounces of whipped butter equals 1 cup.

Low-fat spreads contain a higher proportion of water and air, and their performance as a baking ingredient is unpredictable. For best results, follow the recipes as written. If you wish to experiment with reduced-fat spreads to lower the fat content of baked goods, make gradual modifications to the recipe and see how you like the results. The finished product will likely have a slightly tougher texture and less browned exterior. You may enjoy lower-fat muffins better if you modify an unfamiliar recipe rather than a tried-and-true family favorite whose altered form may be disappointing.

Vegetable oil provides tenderness and moisture in many muffin and quick bread recipes; oil and butter are not interchangeable because they react differently with the other ingredients. Corn oil is a good all-purpose oil for muffins and quick breads; don't substitute olive oil, which has too strong a flavor.

Nonstick cooking spray is oil in a pressurized can that makes it possible to disperse a thin, fine layer. It is convenient for greasing pans and paper liners.

Baking Powder and Baking Soda

Either or both of these are used as leaveners for many muffins and quick breads. Baking soda also helps neutralize acidic ingredients. For best results when using baking powder, check the expiration date stamped on the bottom of the package and replace outdated product. Do not substitute one for the other, as they interact differently with other ingredients.

Dairy Products

Milk provides flavor and tenderness and helps promote browning, too. Most recipes work equally well made with whole, low-fat or skim milk, so use what you have on hand or what your dietary needs dictate.

Dried milk powder is a useful, shelf-stable substitute for fresh milk. Even if you wouldn't drink a glass of the reconstituted powder, you'd need an extremely discerning palate to be able to tell if a baked recipe was made with powdered or fresh milk. Substitute reconstituted milk equally for fresh. Even easier, substitute water for milk with the wet ingredients, then stir in the corresponding amount of milk powder with the dry ingredients. If you're looking to boost protein or calcium intake, double the amount of milk powder. It will enhance nutritional benefits without affecting flavor or texture.

Buttermilk has the same nutritional profile of skim milk and is especially good in muffins and quick breads, adding tenderness and a bit of tang. Purchase buttermilk in the dairy section of the supermarket or improvise by mixing 1 tablespoon vinegar or lemon juice with milk to make 1 cup. Let the mixture stand for about 10 minutes. It will look lumpy and curdled, which is perfect! Muffin and quick bread recipes that call for buttermilk require baking soda as the leavener to neutralize the acid in the buttermilk. If you substitute buttermilk for regular milk in a recipe, add ½ teaspoon baking soda with the dry ingredients for every 1 cup buttermilk used.

Sour cream and yogurt, like buttermilk, contribute flavor and tenderness. Sour cream yields a richer coffee cake or muffin than yogurt, but, unless products are consumed side by side, most people can't tell the difference. Pour the liquid off from the top of the yogurt before measuring. As with buttermilk, sour cream and yogurt require baking soda to neutralize the acid.

Eggs

The recipes in this book have been tested using large eggs. If you use a different size, you will alter the recipe's ingredient proportions and results may differ. Eggs have expiration dates stamped on the carton. Open the package in the supermarket to check for cracked or broken shells before you buy; at home, discard any shells that cracked or broke in transit. Store eggs in the main compartment of the refrigerator, not in the trays in the door, which are subject to many temperature fluctuations as the door is opened and closed.

Sweeteners

Sugar adds sweetness, tenderness and moistness to recipes while it aids in browning. Recipes that simply call for "sugar" mean white, granulated sugar. To measure, scoop sugar into a dry measuring cup and level it off at the top.

Brown sugar is a mixture of granulated sugar and molasses that contributes moistness, color and flavor to recipes. The dark version has a more pronounced flavor than the lighter version. The two may be used interchangeably, though the resulting baked goods will differ slightly. Pack brown sugar firmly into a dry measuring cup and level it at the top.

Powdered sugar, also known as confectioners' sugar, is finely ground granulated sugar that contains cornstarch for ease of mixing and blending. Because it dissolves more readily than granulated sugar, it's most often used in icings and as a final sprinkle. Sift it before use to get rid of lumps.

Honey, like sugar, adds moisture and sweetness, but it also contributes a distinct flavor. To substitute, 1 cup honey equals $1\frac{1}{4}$ cups sugar plus $\frac{1}{4}$ cup liquid.

Molasses, a by-product of sugar refining, is a thick, sweet liquid available in light and dark varieties. It's especially good in gingerbread and other recipes that contain sweet spices such as cinnamon, nutmeg, ginger and cloves. A third variety, blackstrap molasses, is unsuitable for baking because of its bitter taste.

Corn syrup is a thick, sweet liquid that comes in dark and light varieties. It's widely used as a sweetener in commercial products, and occasionally in cookie recipes, too.

Tools and Equipment

Oven Thermometer
Ovens may run slightly hotter or colder than the temperature dial indicates, affecting baking time. Set the thermometer in the oven while it preheats; check the temperature after 15 minutes.

Mixing Bowls
Stainless steel bowls are unbreakable, economical and easy to clean. Crockery or glass bowls allow you to melt butter in the microwave right in the mixing bowl. Plastic bowls are inexpensive but may hold traces of grease despite conscientious cleaning. Don't use plastic to beat egg whites.

Perfect Popovers, page 139

Wooden Spoons

The old-fashioned mixing spoon is all you need for blending most muffins and quick breads. They're easier to hold and quieter than metal spoons for mixing batters.

Electric Mixers

While electric mixers are indispensable for fine-textured coffee cakes, most of the recipes in this book should be mixed by hand, because using an electric mixer can result in overmixing, which will toughen most muffins and quick breads.

Wire Cooling Racks

After you remove hot pans from the oven, cool them on a wire rack to allow air circulation. Remove muffins and quick breads from pans within 10 minutes to prevent soggy bottoms.

Measuring Spoons

Use a proper set for accurate measurement; do not rely on ordinary silverware or estimates.

Liquid and Dry Measuring Cups

Baked goods depend on chemical reactions of precise amounts of ingredients, so you do need both liquid and dry measures. Liquid measuring cups are transparent and, to prevent spills, are slightly bigger than the maximum amount to be measured. Pour the liquid to eye level for most accurate measuring. Dry measuring cups are designed to hold the exact amount called for; level off ingredients with the flat side of a knife or spatula.

Peach 'n Blueberry Coffee Cake, page 207

Baking Tips

Always preheat the oven for at least 10 minutes. Avoid opening the oven door before the minimum baking time has elapsed. Place baking pans in the middle of the oven—not touching the walls—for the best air circulation. If you're placing pans on more than one rack, stagger their placement rather than setting one directly above the other for best airflow.

Making Skinnier Muffins and Quick Breads

All of our recipes include detailed nutrition information to help you decide what best fits your personal eating plan, even if it's the occasional splurge. If cutting fat intake is a priority, you may want to modify some of the recipes. Keep in mind that baking is less tolerant of drastic substitutions than other types of cooking, so you may need to experiment. You will have best results by modifying one ingredient rather than several.

Some tips:

- In most recipes in this book, you can substitute nonfat plain yogurt for sour cream and use skim milk instead of whole.
- Try replacing some of the fat (usually butter or margarine) in a recipe with applesauce, pureed prunes, mashed banana or nonfat plain yogurt, which add moistness, flavor and tenderness. Pureed prunes and mashed banana will change the character of the recipe the most, which may or may not be desirable.
- Reduce the amount of rich add-ins such as nuts or chocolate chips. Instead of stirring whole nuts into the batter, mince a smaller quantity and sprinkle them on top for added flavor with less fat.
- Try substituting egg white or nonfat egg product for whole eggs. Use ¼ cup nonfat egg product for each whole egg.
- A sprinkling of plain or spiced sugar on muffins before baking adds moisture and sweetness with only minimal calories and no fat.
- Raisins and other dried fruits add texture and sweetness but no fat. If desired, soak them in liquid before use; otherwise, they may absorb moisture from the recipe.
- Fat's function in baked goods is to provide flavor, moisture and tenderness. Reduced-fat baked goods are best served warm from the oven (or reheated briefly in the microwave oven) before serving. Top them with fruit preserves, nonfat whipped topping, honey or fresh fruit for added flavor and moisture. Note that reduced-fat baked goods don't keep as well as those with more fat.
- Low-fat muffins stick to paper liners; spray the pans with nonstick cooking spray instead of using paper liners, or spray the paper liners.

Muffin Basics

Muffin Equipment

- Muffin baking requires little in the way of special equipment aside from muffin pans, which may be round or whimsically shaped (e.g., hearts). Whether you prefer regular-sized, jumbo or miniature tins—or muffin-tops pans—inexpensive aluminum muffin pans work just fine. Use paper or foil liners to expedite cleanup.
- If you do not have enough muffin pans, set foil liners in individual custard cups on a cookie sheet; fill with batter. Or, bake the remaining batter in a small loaf pan.
- A spring-lever ice-cream scoop is a tidy way to transfer batter from bowl to tin. Otherwise, use a large spoon, long-handled measuring cup or soup ladle.

Technique Tips

- Most of the muffins in this chapter call for two-bowl preparation. The dry ingredients get mixed in one, stirred thoroughly to distribute salt and leaveners evenly; the wet ingredients (including cooking oil or melted butter) get mixed in a second bowl. Measure ingredients carefully. When it's time to combine wet and dry, be sure to mix gently, just enough to moisten, to keep muffins tender. Overbeating develops gluten, a combination of two proteins in flour that provide structure and elasticity. Gluten development is key for yeast breads, but it toughens muffins.
- A few recipes in this book call for creaming solid butter rather than using liquid fat. This style of muffin is finer grained and has a cake-like texture. You'll have the best results if you let the butter soften before creaming; again, avoid overmixing when combining wet and dry ingredients.
- Fill muffin tins about ⅔ full to allow room for the batter to expand in the oven. If you're going for the "jumbo" muffin effect, grease the tops of the tins, too, to facilitate removal after baking.
- If there's not enough batter to fill all of the cups, pour a little water in the empty cups before baking so that the tin heats evenly.
- Reduced-fat muffins are more likely to stick to muffin paper liners than are conventional muffins. For best results, spray muffin tins with nonstick cooking spray instead of using paper liners, or spray the paper liners. Remove the liners while the muffins are still warm.
- Don't overbake muffins. To test for doneness, insert a toothpick or

cake tester in the center; if it comes out clean, the muffins are done.

- Most homemade muffins, especially if you've chosen a reduced-fat version or modified the recipe, taste best when still warm. To rejuvenate leftover muffins, heat in the microwave or toaster oven just long enough to warm them.

Make-Ahead Muffins

If you love warm-from-the-oven muffins at breakfast, but your mornings are too hectic to make a batter from scratch, make-ahead muffins might be the answer. This chapter includes several recipes that allow you to mix up a bowlful of batter and refrigerate it in a tightly covered container for up to two weeks. In the morning, simply fill the desired number of muffin cups and bake. This is also a great option for couples or small families who can't polish off a dozen of anything before staleness sets in. Make-ahead muffins include:

Bran Muffins, page 28
Fruity Orange Refrigerator Muffins,
    page 74
Refrigerator Apple Bran Muffins,
    page 74
Refrigerator Bran Muffins, page 32
Refrigerator Pumpkin Bran Muffins,
    page 45
Refrigerator Sweet Muffins,
    page 30

Making Muffins into Loaves

Most muffin batters can easily be baked in loaf form. In general, a recipe that calls for about 2 cups of flour and makes a dozen muffins can be baked in a 9 × 5 or 8 × 4-inch loaf pan or a 9-inch square cake pan. You'll need to increase cooking time, though the exact duration depends on the type of recipe and type of pan, etc. To estimate, plan on an additional 10 to 15 minutes for batter baked in the square cake pan; for the loaf pan, baking time may be double.

Easy-Tote Options

Muffins are a welcome change from ordinary bread for a lunchbox or picnic basket, so long as you choose a version that's moist and sturdy enough to transport. Some good choices:

Apricot Sunshine Muffins, page 47
Banana Oat Muffins, page 64
Banana Snack Muffins, page 70
Bran Muffins, page 28
Golden Harvest Muffins, page 48
Pineapple-Macadamia Muffins,
    page 42

Freezing Tips

A cache of already baked muffins can brighten a busy day or be ideal for unexpected company. After baking muffins, cool thoroughly, then pack them in a heavy-duty resealable plastic bag and freeze. If you'll be storing them for longer than a week or two, it's a good idea to wrap each muffin individually in plastic before freezing.

Defrost muffins, still wrapped, at room temperature for several hours. Or, unwrap and reheat them briefly in the microwave oven (try 15 to 30 seconds, testing at 10-second intervals) or in a preheated 350°F. oven for about 10 to 15 minutes.

Commonly Asked Questions About Muffins

Q. Why do my muffins turn out tough with large holes and "tunnels" inside?

A. The batter was probably over-mixed. Mix dry and wet ingredients together gently, just enough to moisten.

Q. What causes homebaked muffins to turn out dry?

A. Your muffins were probably in the oven too long. Baking time can vary depending on the temperature fluctuation of your oven, as well as the amount of batter in each cup, the type of cookware and even the weather. That's why recipes specify a range of baking times. Check the temperature of your oven with an oven thermometer and be sure to test for doneness at the earliest recommended time. They're done as soon as the shape is gently domed and tops are golden brown (though color is not a foolproof indicator—for instance, this won't be true if the muffins are made with chocolate, whole wheat flour, molasses or another dark ingredient). The most reliable way to test is by inserting a toothpick in the center. If it comes out clean (no clinging crumbs or splotches of wet batter), the muffins are done. Don't be fooled by sticking the toothpick into melted chocolate or another gooey ingredient; choose a second test spot.

Q. My muffins come out soggy and heavy. How can I get them to be lighter?

A. There are a few things that may be going wrong. Did you measure carefully? You might have included too much of the wet ingredients (especially "heavy" ones such as mashed banana or applesauce) or too little of the dry. Your baking powder might have expired; check the "use by" date on the package. Underbaked muffins will also be heavy and soggy; if you peeked in the oven too many times while they were trying to rise, you may have interfered with the outcome. Chalk it up to experience and try again.

Quick Bread Basics

Equipment

In addition to the standard kitchen tools, the only special equipment needed to make quick breads are loaf pans. The most common sizes are 9 × 5 and 8 × 4-inch (or substitute a 1-quart casserole dish); smaller pans (e.g., 6 × 3½-inch) make cute miniature loaves. Cornbread and soda bread are often made in 8 or 9-inch square or round cake pans; for thick doughs that make free-form breads, a baking sheet is sometimes used.

Making Muffins from Loaves

You can bake almost any batter from the Quick Breads chapter in muffin tins instead of a loaf pan, or divide the batter for one big loaf into two or three "mini"-loaves. A recipe that uses about 2 cups of flour and makes one 8 × 4 or 9 × 5-inch loaf (or a 9-inch square) will make about a dozen muffins (or a few more, depending on the ingredients called for). Muffins will be done in about half the time of a large loaf. Reduce the baking time accordingly.

Freezing Loaves

Most quick bread loaves freeze well, giving you a head start on holiday baking or a hearty treat during hectic weeks. Cool loaves completely; do not glaze or decorate. Wrap them tightly in plastic wrap or wrap individual slices to thaw more quickly. If you intend to freeze loaves for more than a week, wrap first in plastic wrap, then in aluminum foil. For added protection, place wrapped loaves in a resealable plastic freezer bag. Be sure to label the outside with the type of bread and the date and use within one month.

Unwrap slightly and thaw the loaf at room temperature; glaze or decorate according to the recipe.

Special Toppings

While quick breads don't usually get a thick crown of frosting in the style of layer cakes, a bit of sweetness or crunch on top is often just the right finishing touch. If the recipe doesn't specify a topping, sprinkle the quick breads before baking with:

- Granulated sugar or miniature chocolate chips
- 2 tablespoons sugar mixed with ½ teaspoon cinnamon and/or nutmeg
- 2 tablespoons sugar mixed with 1 tablespoon grated orange or lemon peel
- Minced nuts
- 2 tablespoons sugar blended with 1 teaspoon cinnamon and 2 teaspoons softened butter
- ¼ cup all-purpose flour, rolled oats or crushed bran flakes cereal with 2 tablespoons brown sugar, ½ teaspoon cinnamon and 2 tablespoons softened butter

Loaves and Good Wishes

Holiday loaves are signature gifts in many families. Make sure to label each loaf for the recipient, explaining the type of loaf and indicating if refrigeration is needed. Presentation can be as simple as sticking a bow on the wrapping. For a recent bride or graduate setting up a household, a new loaf pan, a recipe or copy of this book and a few kitchen implements make a thoughtful gift. Some of the recipes in this chapter include other gift suggestions.

Commonly Asked Questions About Quick Breads

Q. The top of my loaf is so cracked, it looks like the San Andreas Fault. What went wrong?

A. That's okay! A crack on top is characteristic of many quick bread loaves. If the crack is very large, the batter may have been over-mixed. Like muffins, most quick breads require gentle handling. Next time, stir just enough to moisten the ingredients.

Q. My loaf looks gorgeous on the outside, but why are there bitter-tasting white lumps inside?

A. Your leavener was probably lumpy. If baking soda or baking powder looks lumpy in the container, press it through a small sieve into the flour mixture and then make sure to stir the dry ingredients thoroughly before blending them with the wet ingredients.

Q. I'm sure my loaf was done; the toothpick came out clean. But now the bread seems very soggy. Why?

A. Make sure there's good air circulation around the loaf as it cools. Set the loaf pan on a wire rack as soon as it comes out of the oven and let the loaf cool in the pan for 10 to 15 minutes; then turn the loaf out onto the rack to cool completely. If the loaf is wrapped too soon or set on a plate or other solid surface, steam rising from the hot loaf will condense as it cools, and beads of moisture will collect inside the wrapper (or on the plate) and cause sogginess.

Q. Why do some recipes turn out tough?

A. Chances are, you mixed the batter with a little too much enthusiasm. Like muffins, most quick breads require gentle handling. Next time, stir just enough to moisten the ingredients.

Coffee Cake Basics

Although the definition of "coffee cakes" sometimes includes yeast cakes, we've chosen quicker, simpler versions, all of which are leavened with baking powder and/or baking soda.

Equipment

Coffee cakes come in all shapes and sizes. The pans you'll need to make the recipes in this chapter include:

- 8 or 9-inch round or square cake pans
- 9 or 10-inch springform pans (the sides of springform pans "latch" to hold the pan tightly around the cake as it bakes, then "unlatch" to free the baked cake)
- 13 × 9-inch cake/brownie pan
- 10-inch tube pan (also known as an angel food cake pan)
- 12-cup Bundt® pan (similar to a tube pan, but with scalloped edges)

Make-Ahead Tips

Coffee cakes are especially popular because most of them keep well, making it possible to prepare them hours or even a day or so ahead of your gathering. If you prefer to bake at the last minute and serve coffee cakes warm, make your own coffee cake "mix" by measuring and blending all of the dry ingredients ahead of time, and organizing all of the liquid ingredients in one spot in the refrigerator.

To freeze coffee cakes, cool them completely; do not frost or decorate. Wrap tightly in heavy-duty plastic wrap and store in the freezer for up to one month. Unwrap slightly and thaw at room temperature for 2 to 3 hours. Or, freeze individual slices and thaw in the microwave oven for a quick treat when a friend drops by.

Blueberry Muffin Cake, page 205

Biscuit Basics

Old-fashioned baking powder biscuits are delightfully versatile—homey enough to round out a family supper yet special enough to serve to company. For best results, make sure to handle the dough with a light touch, then serve the biscuits warm from the oven.

Biscuit recipes usually call for cutting shortening or butter into the flour mixture, as for pastry. The shortening should be somewhat cold so it doesn't completely melt into the dough. Use a pastry blender, a fork or two knives to cut the shortening into the flour mixture until it resembles coarse crumbs. Add the liquid gradually, stirring until the dough just about clings together and follows the spoon. You may not need all the liquid specified; occasionally, you might need a few drops more. You want the dough to be moist enough to hold together, but not so sticky that you can't handle it.

For smoother tops and texture, toss the biscuit dough on a lightly floured work surface and knead it gently for 10 or so turns, just enough to make the dough fairly smooth. Roll or pat it out to the specified thickness, then cut it into circles, squares or diamonds with a biscuit cutter or knife. Some cooks use a drinking glass as a cutter, but this is not ideal as the rounded lip of the glass tends to squash the dough; a sharper edge is preferable.

A shiny aluminum cookie sheet works best for baking, especially if you like crisper biscuits; a cake pan works, too.

For crispy biscuits, leave 1 to 2 inches of space between the biscuits on the baking sheet; for softer sides, nestle the pieces close together so the sides touch.

Bake the biscuits until they're golden brown (for "quality control," break a warm one open to make sure it's cooked through), and transfer them to a basket lined with a cloth kitchen towel. This setup will hold some of the heat in, while allowing enough moisture to escape so the biscuits don't become soggy.

For even greater warmth retention, heat a biscuit stone or unglazed quarry tile in the oven while the biscuits bake, then put it in the bottom of the basket under a hot pad or folded dish towel to serve as a bun warmer.

Tip Talk

Throughout the book, you will find helpful hints accompanying each recipe. The information falls into the following categories.

Recipe Fact

imparts a bit of culinary background.

About (Ingredient)

shares a nugget of information about a component of the recipe.

Kitchen Tip

explains the most expeditious way to prepare certain ingredients or carry out special techniques.

Healthy Hint

recommends easy ways to reduce fat or calories in the recipe.

Ingredient Substitution

proposes satisfactory alternatives in case your pantry lacks a specific item called for in the recipe.

Make-Ahead Tip

tells how much of the preparation can be completed in advance.

Make It Special

offers easy ideas for garnishes and embellishments for the bread.

Recipe Variation

outlines an easy way to transform the recipe at hand into a new and different dish.

Menu Suggestion

lists ideas for dishes to complement the particular recipe.

Storage Tip

suggests how best to keep dough or baked goods fresh.

In addition, four special "flags" help categorize recipes at a glance:

Editor's Favorite gives you insider information about our staff's very favorite recipes.

Fiber Source denotes recipes that have 3 grams of fiber or more per serving.

Gift Idea denotes recipes that are well suited for holiday gifts.

Low-Fat denotes recipes that have 3 grams of fat or less per serving.

Sweet Muffins

Pair fruit-studded muffins with your morning coffee, nibble delicately spiced muffins with a cup of tea in the afternoon, indulge in cake-like muffins for dessert. With 40 recipes ranging from homestyle to highbrow, these muffins go from the baking tin to the table in a trice, ready whenever a meal or snack needs a sweet punctuation.

Sweet Muffins

Previous page: Berry Citrus Muffins, page 25

Berry Citrus Muffins

Prep Time: 15 minutes
(Ready in 40 minutes)

2 cups all-purpose flour
½ cup sugar
3 teaspoons baking powder
1 teaspoon grated lemon or
  orange peel
½ teaspoon salt
½ cup orange juice

½ cup margarine or butter,
  melted
1 egg
¾ cup fresh or frozen
  blueberries (do not thaw)
¾ cup fresh or frozen
  raspberries (do not thaw)

1. Heat oven to 400°F. Line 12 muffin cups with paper baking cups or grease bottoms only. In large bowl, combine flour, sugar, baking powder, lemon peel and salt; mix well.

2. In small bowl, combine orange juice, margarine and egg; blend well. Add to flour mixture; stir just until dry ingredients are moistened. (Batter will be very thick.) Gently stir in berries. Divide batter evenly into paper-lined muffin cups, filling each ¾ full.

3. Bake at 400°F. for 18 to 25 minutes or until muffins are light golden brown and toothpick inserted in center comes out clean. Cool 1 minute; remove from pan. Serve warm.

Yield: 12 muffins
High Altitude (Above 3,500 Feet): Decrease baking powder to 2 teaspoons.
Bake as directed above.

Nutrition Information Per Serving
Serving Size: 1 Muffin. Calories 200 • Calories from Fat 70 • Total Fat 8 g •
Saturated Fat 2 g • Cholesterol 20 mg • Sodium 310 mg • Dietary Fiber 1 g
Dietary Exchanges: 1 Starch, 1 Fruit, 1½ Fat OR 2 Carbohydrate, 1½ Fat

About Salt

Unless you have a medical problem with sodium intake, don't leave out the salt from Berry Citrus Muffins or other muffins and quick breads. Salt rounds out flavors, even in sweet foods, and baked goods that lack it taste curiously "flat" and bland.

Recipe Variation

Make the muffins with cranberries instead of either the blueberries or raspberries.

Storage Tip

Fresh raspberries are highly perishable, which is one reason they're usually expensive. Plan to use them within a day of purchase. In the meantime, keep them refrigerated, loosely covered in the original carton or in a dish lined with a paper towel to absorb moisture, to prevent the all-too-quick growth of mold.

Basic Muffins

Recipe Fact

Here's the basic muffin: an honest, straightforward treat that's sweeter than a biscuit but not as rich as a cake. From this starting point, try the sweet variations that follow or invent your own.

Kitchen Tip

The traditional bread basket lined with a clean kitchen towel is still the ideal way to serve warm-from-the-oven muffins. The towel holds in some warmth while the open weave of the basket lets steam escape, which could otherwise condense and make the muffins soggy.

Prep Time: 10 minutes
(Ready in 35 minutes)

2 cups all-purpose flour	**³/₄ cup milk**
¹/₂ cup sugar	**¹/₃ cup oil**
3 teaspoons baking powder	**1 egg, beaten**
¹/₂ teaspoon salt	

1. Heat oven to 400°F. Grease bottoms only of 12 muffin cups or line with paper baking cups. In medium bowl, combine flour, sugar, baking powder and salt; mix well.
2. In small bowl, combine milk, oil and egg; beat well. Add to flour mixture all at once; stir just until dry ingredients are moistened. (Batter will be lumpy.) Divide batter evenly into greased muffin cups.
3. Bake at 400°F. for 20 to 25 minutes or until toothpick inserted in center comes out clean. Cool 1 minute; remove from pan. Serve warm.

Yield: 12 muffins
High Altitude (Above 3,500 Feet): No change.

Tip: *To substitute for buttermilk, use 2 tablespoons and 1½ teaspoons vinegar or lemon juice plus milk to make 2½ cups.

Nutrition Information Per Serving
Serving Size: 1 Muffin. Calories 180 • Calories from Fat 60 • Total Fat 7 g • Saturated Fat 1 g • Cholesterol 20 mg • Sodium 220 mg • Dietary Fiber 1 g Dietary Exchanges: 1 Starch, ½ Fruit, 1½ Fat OR 1½ Carbohydrate, 1½ Fat

---

Variations

Apple Muffins: Decrease sugar to ¼ cup; add 1 teaspoon cinnamon to flour. Stir 1 cup finely chopped, peeled apple into dry ingredients. Substitute apple juice for milk. Bake at 400°F. for 18 to 22 minutes.

Blueberry Muffins: Stir 1 cup fresh or frozen blueberries (do not thaw) and 1 teaspoon grated lemon or orange peel into dry ingredients.

Chocolate Chip Muffins: Add ¾ cup miniature chocolate chips with flour. Before baking, sprinkle batter in cups with a combination of 3 tablespoons sugar and 2 tablespoons brown sugar.

Jam Muffins: Place ½ teaspoon any flavor jam on each muffin before baking; press into batter. If desired, sprinkle with finely chopped nuts.

Lemon Muffins: Add 1 tablespoon grated lemon peel with flour.

Orange Muffins: Add 1 tablespoon grated orange peel with flour; substitute orange juice for milk.

Streusel-Topped Muffins: In small bowl, combine ¼ cup firmly packed brown sugar, 1 tablespoon softened margarine or butter, ½ teaspoon cinnamon and ¼ cup chopped nuts or flaked coconut; stir with fork until crumbly. Sprinkle evenly over batter in cups before baking.

Sugar-Coated Muffins: After baking, brush tops of hot muffins with 2 tablespoons melted margarine or butter; dip in mixture of ¼ cup sugar and ½ teaspoon cinnamon.

Whole Wheat Muffins: Use 1 cup all-purpose flour and 1 cup whole wheat flour.

Bran Muffins

Recipe Fact

Bran muffins have a healthy reputation because bran adds beneficial dietary fiber to the batter. Don't be fooled, however; some commercially available bran muffins (especially those tempting jumbo-sized ones) can contain up to 500 calories apiece, and quite a few fat grams. Our recipe weighs in at a reasonable 150 calories— about the same as two slices of bread.

Recipe Variation

Add grated rind of ½ orange and ½ cup chopped walnuts to the batter before baking.

2 cups shreds of whole bran cereal
2½ cups buttermilk*
½ cup oil
2 eggs
2½ cups all-purpose flour
1½ cups sugar
1¼ teaspoons baking soda
1 teaspoon baking powder
½ teaspoon salt
¾ cup raisins, if desired

1. In large bowl, combine cereal and buttermilk; mix well. Let stand 5 minutes until cereal is softened. Add oil and eggs; blend well.
2. Add all remaining ingredients; mix well. Batter can be baked immediately or stored in tightly covered container in refrigerator for up to 2 weeks.
3. When ready to bake, heat oven to 400°F. Grease desired number of muffin cups or line with paper baking cups. Stir batter; fill greased muffin cups ¾ full.
4. Bake at 400°F. for 18 to 20 minutes or until toothpick inserted in center comes out clean. Immediately remove from pan. Serve warm.

Yield: 30 muffins
High Altitude (Above 3,500 Feet): Increase flour to 2¾ cups;
decrease sugar to 1¼ cups. Bake as directed above.

Tip: *To substitute for buttermilk, use 2 tablespoons and 1½ teaspoons vinegar or lemon juice plus milk to make 2½ cups.

Nutrition Information Per Serving
Serving Size: 1 Muffin. Calories 150 • Calories from Fat 35 • Total Fat 4 g • Saturated Fat 1 g • Cholesterol 15 mg • Sodium 140 mg • Dietary Fiber 2 g
Dietary Exchanges: 1 Starch, ½ Fruit, ½ Fat OR 1½ Carbohydrate, ½ Fat

Bran Muffins

Refrigerator Sweet Muffins

Prep Time: 10 minutes
(Ready in 35 minutes)

4½ cups all-purpose flour	1 teaspoon salt
1 cup firmly packed brown sugar	2 cups buttermilk*
½ cup sugar	¾ cup oil
4 teaspoons baking powder	1½ teaspoons vanilla
1 teaspoon baking soda	3 eggs

1. In large bowl, combine flour, brown sugar, sugar, baking powder, baking soda and salt; mix well. Add buttermilk, oil, vanilla and eggs; stir just until dry ingredients are moistened. Batter can be baked immediately or stored in tightly covered container in refrigerator for up to 5 days.

2. When ready to bake, heat oven to 375°F. Grease bottoms only of desired number of muffin cups or line with paper baking cups. Stir batter; fill greased muffin cups ⅔ full.

3. Bake at 375°F. for 20 to 25 minutes or until toothpick inserted in center comes out clean. Immediately remove from pan. Serve warm.

Yield: 24 muffins
High Altitude (Above 3,500 Feet): Decrease brown sugar to ¾ cup. Bake as directed above.

Tip: *To substitute for buttermilk, use 2 tablespoons vinegar or lemon juice plus milk to make 2 cups.

Nutrition Information Per Serving
Serving Size: 1 Muffin. Calories 220 • Calories from Fat 70 • Total Fat 8 g • Saturated Fat 1 g • Cholesterol 25 mg • Sodium 260 mg • Dietary Fiber 1 g
Dietary Exchanges: 1½ Starch, ½ Fruit, 1½ Fat OR 2 Carbohydrate, 1½ Fat

---

Variations

Chocolate Chip: Fold in ⅓ cup miniature semi-sweet chocolate chips.

Cinnamon Topped: After baking, dip top of each muffin in melted butter, then in a mixture of 2 tablespoons sugar, ¼ teaspoon cinnamon and ⅛ teaspoon nutmeg.

Maple Walnut: Fold in ⅓ cup chopped walnuts and ½ teaspoon maple extract.

Mixed Fruit: Fold in ⅓ cup chopped dried mixed fruit.

Pineapple Coconut: Fold in ⅓ cup drained, crushed pineapple and ¼ cup coconut.

Refrigerator Sweet Muffins

Refrigerator Bran Muffins

Prep Time: 10 minutes
(Ready in 35 minutes)

2½ cups buttermilk*
⅓ cup oil
2 eggs
3 cups bran flakes cereal with
  or without raisins

2½ cups all-purpose flour
1 cup sugar
1¼ teaspoons baking soda
1 teaspoon baking powder
½ teaspoon salt

About Refrigerator Muffins

Refrigerator muffins combine homemade flavor with premixed convenience. They're equally handy for small families who can't finish a batch of muffins before they become stale and large families looking to streamline last-minute prep. The batter keeps in the refrigerator (in a tightly covered container) for up to two weeks. As needed, you can bake the desired number of muffins.

About Double-Acting Baking Powder

The secret to refrigerated muffin batters is the double-acting baking powder. It reacts first with liquids and then with heat during baking. Because baking powder loses its ability to leaven baked goods over time, use it before the expiration date on the package.

Recipe Variation

Substitute 2½ cups orange juice for the buttermilk, and add 1 teaspoon grated orange peel to the batter.

1. In large bowl, combine buttermilk, oil and eggs; beat well. Add all remaining ingredients; stir just until dry ingredients are moistened. Batter can be baked immediately or stored in tightly covered container in refrigerator for up to 2 weeks.

2. When ready to bake, heat oven to 400°F. Line desired number of muffin cups with paper baking cups. Stir batter; fill paper-lined muffin cups ⅔ full.

3. Bake at 400°F. for 20 to 25 minutes or until toothpick inserted in center comes out clean. Immediately remove from pan. Serve warm.

Yield: 30 muffins
High Altitude (Above 3,500 Feet): Increase flour to 3 cups. Bake as directed above.

Tip: *To substitute for buttermilk, use 2 tablespoons and 1½ teaspoons vinegar or lemon juice plus milk to make 2½ cups.

Nutrition Information Per Serving

Serving Size: 1 Muffin. Calories 120 • Calories from Fat 25 • Total Fat 3 g • Saturated Fat 1 g • Cholesterol 15 mg • Sodium 160 mg • Dietary Fiber 1 g Dietary Exchanges: 1 Starch, ½ Fruit, ½ Fat OR 1½ Carbohydrate, ½ Fat

---

Honey-Glazed Banana Bran Muffins

Prep Time: 20 minutes
(Ready in 45 minutes)

Muffins

2 cups shreds of whole bran
  cereal
1 cup buttermilk*
½ cup (1 medium) mashed ripe
  banana
¼ cup oil
¼ cup honey
1 egg, slightly beaten

1 cup whole wheat flour
1 teaspoon baking soda
⅛ teaspoon salt

Glaze

2 tablespoons margarine or
  butter, softened
2 tablespoons honey

1. Heat oven to 400°F. Line 16 muffin cups with paper baking cups. In large bowl, combine cereal and buttermilk; mix well. Let stand 10 minutes until cereal is softened.
2. Add banana, oil, honey and egg; blend well. Add flour, baking soda and salt; stir just until dry ingredients are moistened. Fill paper-lined muffin cups ⅔ full.
3. Bake at 400°F. for 18 to 22 minutes or until toothpick inserted in center comes out clean.
4. Meanwhile, in small bowl, blend glaze ingredients until smooth. Set aside.
5. Immediately brush hot muffins with glaze. Remove from pan. Serve warm.

Yield: 16 muffins
High Altitude (Above 3,500 Feet): No change.

Tip: *To substitute for buttermilk, use 1 tablespoon vinegar or lemon juice plus milk to make 1 cup.

Nutrition Information Per Serving

Serving Size: 1 Muffin. Calories 160 • Calories from Fat 50 • Total Fat 6 g •
Saturated Fat 1 g • Cholesterol 15 mg • Sodium 150 mg • Dietary Fiber 5 g
Dietary Exchanges: 1 Starch, ½ Fruit, 1 Fat OR 1½ Carbohydrate, 1 Fat

---

Healthy Hint

Recipes made with mashed bananas are often a good choice for someone with a sweet tooth who's nonetheless trying to cut down on fat. Bananas add moisture, sweetness and texture, compensating for the reduced fat.

Kitchen Tip

Honey lasts indefinitely, but sometimes becomes crystallized. To recoup the smooth, pourable consistency, remove the cover and place the jar in a pan of hot or simmering water until the crystals melt.

Queen's Muffins

Prep Time: 20 minutes
(Ready in 55 minutes)

1 cup sugar
1 cup margarine or butter,
  softened
3 eggs
1 teaspoon lemon extract
1 teaspoon orange extract

2 cups all-purpose flour
2 teaspoons baking powder
½ teaspoon cinnamon
1 (10-oz.) pkg. dried currants
2 tablespoons powdered sugar

1. Heat oven to 325°F. Line 18 muffin cups with paper baking cups. In large bowl, combine sugar and margarine; beat until light and fluffy. Add eggs 1 at a time, beating well after each addition. Add lemon and orange extracts; beat well.

2. Gradually add flour, baking powder and cinnamon; stir just until dry ingredients are moistened. Stir in currants. Divide batter evenly into muffin cups, filling each ¾ full.

3. Bake at 325°F. for 25 to 30 minutes or until toothpick inserted in center comes out clean. Immediately remove from pan; cool 5 minutes. Sprinkle with powdered sugar. Serve warm.

Yield: 18 muffins
High Altitude (Above 3,500 Feet): Increase flour to 2¼ cups. Bake as directed above.

Nutrition Information Per Serving
Serving Size: 1 Muffin. Calories 250 • Calories from Fat 100 • Total Fat 11 g • Saturated Fat 2 g • Cholesterol 35 mg • Sodium 190 mg • Dietary Fiber 1 g Dietary Exchanges: 1 Starch, 1½ Fruit, 2 Fat OR 2½ Carbohydrate, 2 Fat

Recipe Fact

Worthy of royalty, these extra-rich muffins are made with a full cup of margarine or butter and 3 whole eggs. For the best flavor, use real butter, not margarine.

Menu Suggestion

Serve these tender muffins as part of a traditional British afternoon tea, along with delicate cucumber sandwiches, scones and small dishes of jam, softened butter and whipped cream. Instead of microwaving a mug of water with a tea bag, make tea the authentic way: in a teapot, using two or three tea bags or a tea ball of loose tea. Bring a kettle of fresh, cold water just to a boil, and then pour immediately in the teapot. Let the tea steep for a few minutes until it's the desired strength, then remove the tea bags (don't squeeze the tea bags—those last few drops of tannic acid may impart bitterness).

Queen's Muffins

Raspberry-Lemon Muffins with Streusel Topping

Kitchen Tip

When purchasing muffin tins, look for pans that have cups pressed from one seamless piece of metal. Indentations and grooves around the muffin cups can collect batter and be more of a nuisance to clean.

Ingredient Substitution

Orange juice and peel may be used in place of lemon, and blueberries or chopped fresh cranberries can replace the raspberries.

Recipe Variation

For a muffin with an intriguing flavor, stir ½ teaspoon ground coriander into the muffin batter.

Prep Time: 15 minutes
(Ready in 35 minutes)

Muffins
½ cup low-fat vanilla yogurt
3 tablespoons oil
1 tablespoon fresh lemon juice
2 egg whites
1½ cups all-purpose flour
¾ cup sugar
2 teaspoons baking powder
1 teaspoon grated lemon peel
¼ teaspoon salt
1 cup frozen whole raspberries
(not in syrup)

Streusel Topping
¼ cup sugar
2 tablespoons all-purpose flour
1 tablespoon margarine or butter

1. Heat oven to 400°F. Spray bottoms only of 12 muffin cups with nonstick cooking spray. In small bowl, combine yogurt, oil, lemon juice and egg whites; blend well.
2. In medium bowl, combine 1½ cups flour, ¾ cup sugar, baking powder, lemon peel and salt; mix well. Stir in frozen raspberries.
3. Add yogurt mixture to flour mixture; stir just until dry ingredients are moistened. Spoon batter evenly into sprayed muffin cups.
4. In small bowl, combine all topping ingredients with fork until crumbly; sprinkle evenly over batter in cups before baking.
5. Bake at 400°F. for 16 to 20 minutes or until muffins are golden brown and toothpick inserted in center comes out clean. Immediately remove from pan. Serve warm.

Yield: 12 muffins
High Altitude (Above 3,500 Feet): No change.

Nutrition Information Per Serving
Serving Size: 1 Muffin. Calories 190 • Calories from Fat 45 • Total Fat 5 g •
Saturated Fat 1 g • Cholesterol 0 mg • Sodium 150 mg • Dietary Fiber 1 g
Dietary Exchanges: 1 Starch, 1 Fruit, 1 Fat OR 2 Carbohydrate, 1 Fat

Raspberry-Lemon Muffins with Streusel Topping

Delicate Pear Muffins

About Bartlett Pears

The Bartlett pear, with its juicy, mild flesh, is an all-purpose pear that's delicious eaten out of hand and also good for baking. When a Bartlett is ripe, the skin will be golden and gently speckled, and the neck end will yield to slight pressure.

Kitchen Tip

Peel the pears just before they're needed so they don't discolor.

Recipe Variation

Add 1 tablespoon of grated lemon peel to the batter, too.

Prep Time: 20 minutes
(Ready in 40 minutes)

Muffins
1¾ cups all-purpose flour
⅓ cup sugar
3 teaspoons baking powder
¼ teaspoon salt
¼ teaspoon nutmeg
2 cups (2 medium) cubed
   peeled pears
½ cup skim milk
3 tablespoons oil
1 egg

Topping
3 tablespoons sugar
1 teaspoon finely grated lemon
   peel

1. Heat oven to 400°F. Line 12 muffin cups with paper baking cups and lightly spray with nonstick cooking spray, or spray 12 muffin cups. In large bowl, combine flour, ⅓ cup sugar, baking powder, salt and nutmeg; mix well. Add pears; toss to coat.
2. In small bowl, combine milk, oil and egg; beat well. Add to flour mixture; stir just until dry ingredients are moistened. DO NOT OVERMIX. Divide batter evenly into paper-lined muffin cups.
3. In small bowl, combine topping ingredients; mix well. Sprinkle evenly over batter in cups.
4. Bake at 400°F. for 15 to 20 minutes or until toothpick inserted in center comes out clean and edges are golden brown. Immediately remove from pan. Serve warm.

Yield: 12 muffins
High Altitude (Above 3,500 Feet): No change.

Nutrition Information Per Serving
Serving Size: 1 Muffin. Calories 160 • Calories from Fat 35 • Total Fat 4 g •
Saturated Fat 1 g • Cholesterol 20 mg • Sodium 180 mg • Dietary Fiber 1 g
Dietary Exchanges: 1 Starch, 1 Fruit, ½ Fat OR 2 Carbohydrate, ½ Fat

Pineapple-Carrot Muffins

Prep Time: 20 minutes
(Ready in 50 minutes)

1 cup all-purpose flour
¾ cup whole wheat flour
½ cup firmly packed brown
    sugar
1 teaspoon baking soda
1 teaspoon cinnamon
¼ teaspoon salt
½ cup oil

1 (8-oz.) can crushed pineapple
    in unsweetened juice,
    undrained
1 egg
1 cup shredded carrots
½ cup raisins
½ cup chopped walnuts

1. Heat oven to 375°F. Grease bottoms only of 16 muffin cups or line with paper baking cups. In large bowl, combine all-purpose flour, whole wheat flour, brown sugar, baking soda, cinnamon and salt; mix well.

2. In small bowl, combine oil, pineapple and egg; blend well. Add to flour mixture; stir just until dry ingredients are moistened. Stir in carrots, raisins and walnuts. Fill greased muffin cups ¾ full.

3. Bake at 375°F. for 18 to 22 minutes or until muffins are light brown and toothpick inserted in center comes out clean. Cool 5 minutes; remove from pan. Serve warm.

Yield: 16 muffins
High Altitude (Above 3,500 Feet): Increase all-purpose flour to 1¼ cups.
Bake as directed above.

Nutrition Information Per Serving

Serving Size: 1 Muffin. Calories 200 • Calories from Fat 90 • Total Fat 10 g •
Saturated Fat 1 g • Cholesterol 15 mg • Sodium 75 mg • Dietary Fiber 2 g
Dietary Exchanges: 1 Starch, ½ Fruit, 2 Fat OR 1½ Carbohydrate, 2 Fat

Recipe Fact

Popular carrot cake flavor is packed into these moist muffins, which are sweet enough to double as breakfast or teatime treats or an after-dinner dessert. Ready-to-spread cream cheese frosting makes a tasty topping.

Kitchen Tip

If you're grating carrots by hand, grate the fat end of the carrot first. The tender tip will be easier to grate when you're down to a nubbin. Or, the cook can munch it as a bonus.

Orange-Macadamia Nut Muffins

Prep Time: 15 minutes
(Ready in 35 minutes)

Muffins
2 cups all-purpose flour
2 tablespoons sugar
3 teaspoons baking powder
½ teaspoon salt
1 cup orange juice
3 tablespoons oil
2 teaspoons grated orange peel
2 egg whites

Topping
¼ cup macadamia nuts, finely chopped
2 tablespoons brown sugar
½ teaspoon all-purpose flour

1. Heat oven to 400°F. Spray 12 muffin cups with non-stick cooking spray, or line cups with paper baking cups and spray paper cups. In large bowl, combine 2 cups flour, sugar, baking powder and salt; mix well.
2. In small bowl, combine orange juice, oil, orange peel and egg whites; blend well. Add to flour mixture all at once; stir just until dry ingredients are moistened. Divide batter evenly into sprayed muffin cups.
3. In small bowl, combine all topping ingredients; mix well. Spoon evenly onto batter in cups, pressing in lightly with back of spoon.
4. Bake at 400°F. for 14 to 18 minutes or until muffins are light golden brown and toothpick inserted in center comes out clean. Immediately remove from pan; cool slightly. Serve warm or at room temperature.

Yield: 12 muffins
High Altitude (Above 3,500 Feet): No change.

Nutrition Information Per Serving
Serving Size: 1 Muffin. Calories 150 • Calories from Fat 45 • Total Fat 5 g •
Saturated Fat 1 g • Cholesterol 0 mg • Sodium 220 mg • Dietary Fiber 1 g
Dietary Exchanges: 1 Starch, ½ Fruit, 1 Fat OR 1½ Carbohydrate, 1 Fat

About Macadamia Nuts

Macadamia nuts are a signature crop of Hawaii, though they're actually native to Australia. The roundish, creamy-colored nuts are distinctive and sweet. They're one of the more expensive nuts on the market.

Ingredient Substitution

Substitute walnuts for the macadamias as dictated by budget and availability.

Make It Special

Drizzle muffin tops with melted white baking chips just before serving.

Orange-Macadamia Nut Muffins

Pineapple-Macadamia Muffins

gift idea

About Gingerroot

Fresh gingerroot is knobby and gnarly and certainly won't win any beauty contests. But its unmistakable flavor adds pungent, sweet-hot spiciness to sweet and savory recipes alike. Purchase plump-looking, smooth-skinned fresh ginger and store it at room temperature. Before using, peel off the thin brown skin with a sharp paring knife or vegetable peeler. The flesh is very stringy.

Kitchen Tip

Don't discard the liquid that you drain away from the canned pineapple. Stir it into a fruit salad or shake, or freeze it in ice-cube trays for fruit-flavored cubes. Or, simply drink it!

Ingredient Substitutions

Chopped almonds or walnuts can be used as an alternative to macadamias.

To substitute for buttermilk, use 2 teaspoons vinegar or lemon juice plus milk to make ⅔ cup.

Prep Time: 25 minutes
(Ready in 45 minutes)

½ teaspoon baking soda
⅔ cup buttermilk
⅓ cup finely chopped dry-roasted macadamia nuts
2 tablespoons brown sugar
½ cup firmly packed brown sugar
1 (20-oz.) can crushed pineapple, well drained, reserving 2 tablespoons liquid
½ cup unsweetened applesauce
2 tablespoons oil
½ teaspoon grated gingerroot or ½ teaspoon ginger
1 egg
1½ cups all-purpose flour
1 cup whole wheat flour
3 teaspoons baking powder
1 teaspoon salt

1. Heat oven to 375°F. Spray 18 muffin cups with non-stick cooking spray or line with paper baking cups. In medium bowl, combine baking soda and buttermilk; blend well. Set aside. In small bowl, combine macadamia nuts and 2 tablespoons brown sugar; mix well. Set aside.
2. To buttermilk mixture, add ½ cup brown sugar, pineapple and reserved liquid, applesauce, oil, gingerroot and egg; blend well.
3. In large bowl, combine all-purpose flour, whole wheat flour, baking powder and salt; mix well. Add pineapple mixture; stir just until dry ingredients are moistened. Fill muffin cups ⅔ to ¾ full. Sprinkle about 1 teaspoon nut mixture over batter in each cup.
4. Bake at 375°F. for 15 to 18 minutes or until toothpick inserted in center comes out clean. Immediately remove from pan; cool slightly. Serve warm.

Yield: 18 muffins
High Altitude (Above 3,500 Feet): No change.

Nutrition Information Per Serving
Serving Size: 1 Muffin. Calories 150 • Calories from Fat 35 • Total Fat 4 g •
Saturated Fat 1 g • Cholesterol 10 mg • Sodium 250 mg • Dietary Fiber 2 g
Dietary Exchanges: 1 Starch, ½ Fruit, 1 Fat OR 1½ Carbohydrate, 1 Fat

Sweet Potato Muffins

Prep Time: 20 minutes
(Ready in 40 minutes)

Muffins

1½ cups all-purpose flour
½ cup firmly packed brown
sugar
2 teaspoons baking powder
1 teaspoon baking soda
1 teaspoon pumpkin pie spice
½ teaspoon salt
2 teaspoons grated orange
peel

1 cup mashed canned sweet
potatoes (drained, if
necessary)
½ cup buttermilk
1 tablespoon molasses
2 eggs

Topping

1 tablespoon sugar
¼ teaspoon cinnamon

Ingredient Substitutions

The muffins can also be
made with canned pump-
kin instead of the sweet
potatoes.

To substitute for butter-
milk, use 1½ teaspoons
vinegar or lemon juice
plus milk to make ½ cup.

Recipe Variation

Stir 2 tablespoons minced
crystallized ginger into
the muffin batter.

1. Heat oven to 375°F. Spray 12 muffin cups with nonstick cooking spray, or line with paper baking cups and
lightly spray paper cups. In large bowl, combine flour,
brown sugar, baking powder, baking soda, pumpkin pie
spice, salt and orange peel; mix well.

2. In medium bowl, combine all remaining muffin ingredients; blend well. Add to flour mixture; stir just until dry
ingredients are moistened. Divide batter evenly into
sprayed muffin cups.

3. In small bowl, combine sugar and cinnamon; mix well.
Sprinkle evenly over batter in cups.

4. Bake at 375°F. for 15 to 20 minutes or until toothpick
inserted in center comes out clean. Immediately remove
from pan. Serve warm.

Yield: 12 muffins
High Altitude (Above 3,500 Feet): Increase flour to 1½ cups plus 2 tablespoons.
Bake as directed above.

Nutrition Information Per Serving
Serving Size: 1 Muffin. Calories 140 • Calories from Fat 10 • Total Fat 1 g •
Saturated Fat 0 g • Cholesterol 35 mg • Sodium 320 mg • Dietary Fiber 1 g
Dietary Exchanges: 1 Starch, 1 Fruit OR 2 Carbohydrate

Cheese-Topped Pumpkin Muffins

Recipe Fact

A lump of cream cheese, hidden inside each muffin, becomes a luscious surprise center that hints at the luxury of cheesecake.

About Canned Pumpkin

Canned pumpkin comes in two versions, so read labels carefully. Thanksgiving pies are often made with pumpkin pie filling, which contains spices and may be sweetened. This recipe uses canned pumpkin, which is simply pumpkin that's cooked, then canned without being sweetened or seasoned.

Ingredient Substitution

If pumpkin pie spice isn't available, add 1 teaspoon cinnamon plus a dash each of ground nutmeg, cloves and allspice.

Prep Time: 30 minutes

1¾ cups all-purpose flour
½ cup sugar
3 teaspoons baking powder
1 teaspoon pumpkin pie spice
¼ teaspoon salt
¾ cup canned pumpkin
½ cup skim milk

¼ cup oil
2 egg whites
4 oz. fat-free cream cheese (from 8-oz. pkg.), cut into 12 cubes*
2 tablespoons brown sugar

1. Heat oven to 400°F. Spray 12 muffin cups with nonstick cooking spray, or line muffin cups with paper baking cups and spray cups with nonstick cooking spray.
2. In large bowl, combine flour, sugar, baking powder, pumpkin pie spice and salt; mix well.
3. In small bowl, combine pumpkin, milk, oil and egg whites; blend well. Add to flour mixture all at once; stir just until dry ingredients are moistened. Spoon batter evenly into sprayed muffin cups. Press 1 cube cream cheese into center of each muffin. Top each with ½ teaspoon brown sugar.
4. Bake at 400°F. for 14 to 18 minutes or until toothpick inserted near center, but not into cream cheese, comes out clean. Immediately remove from pan. Serve warm. Store in refrigerator.

Yield: 12 muffins
High Altitude (Above 3,500 Feet): Increase flour to 1¾ cups plus 2 tablespoons.
Divide batter evenly into 14 sprayed muffin cups. Bake at 400°F. for 16 to 20 minutes.

Tip: *Fat-free cream cheese in a tub can be used. Make indentation in center of each muffin with tip of spoon; place 1½ teaspoons cream cheese in each indentation.

Nutrition Information Per Serving

Serving Size: 1 Muffin. Calories 170 • Calories from Fat 45 • Total Fat 5 g • Saturated Fat 1 g • Cholesterol 0 mg • Sodium 240 mg • Dietary Fiber 1 g Dietary Exchanges: 1½ Starch, 1 Fat OR 1½ Carbohydrate, 1 Fat

Refrigerator Pumpkin Bran Muffins

Prep Time: 20 minutes
(Ready in 45 minutes)

2 cups shreds of whole bran cereal	1½ cups sugar
1½ cups buttermilk	1 teaspoon baking powder
1 cup canned pumpkin	1 teaspoon baking soda
½ cup oil	1 teaspoon cinnamon
2 teaspoons grated orange peel	½ teaspoon salt
2 eggs	¼ teaspoon cloves
2½ cups all-purpose flour	¼ teaspoon allspice
	½ cup chopped nuts, if desired
	3 tablespoons sugar

1. In large bowl, combine cereal and buttermilk; mix well. Let stand 5 minutes until cereal is softened.
2. To cereal mixture, add pumpkin, oil, orange peel and eggs; blend well. Add flour, 1½ cups sugar, baking powder, baking soda, cinnamon, salt, cloves, allspice and nuts; mix well. Batter can be baked immediately or stored in tightly covered container in refrigerator for up to 2 weeks.
3. When ready to bake, heat oven to 400°F. Grease desired number of muffin cups or line with paper baking cups. Stir batter; fill greased muffin cups ¾ full. Sprinkle about ¼ teaspoon sugar over batter in each cup.
4. Bake at 400°F. for 18 to 22 minutes or until toothpick inserted in center comes out clean. Immediately remove from pan. Serve warm.

Yield: 30 muffins
High Altitude (Above 3,500 Feet): Decrease sugar in batter to 1¼ cups.
Bake as directed above.

Nutrition Information Per Serving
Serving Size: 1 Muffin. Calories 170 • Calories from Fat 50 • Total Fat 6 g •
Saturated Fat 1 g • Cholesterol 15 mg • Sodium 125 mg • Dietary Fiber 3 g
Dietary Exchanges: 1 Starch, ½ Fruit, 1 Fat OR 1½ Carbohydrate, 1 Fat

fiber source • gift idea

About Double-Acting Baking Powder

The secret to refrigerated muffin batters is the double-acting baking powder. It reacts first with liquids and then with heat during baking. Because baking powder loses its ability to leaven baked goods over time, use it before the expiration date on the package.

Ingredient Substitution

To substitute for buttermilk, use 1 tablespoon plus 1½ teaspoons vinegar or lemon juice plus milk to make 1½ cups.

Recipe Variation

Substitute 1½ cups orange juice for the buttermilk, and add 1 teaspoon grated orange peel to the batter.

Brown Bread Muffin Gems

Recipe Fact

Although there are no eggs or oil in these whole wheat muffins, they're still very moist and flavorful. The muffins are reminiscent of Boston brown bread, a dark brown, molasses-rich specialty that's traditionally steamed on the stove-top and served with Boston baked beans.

Ingredient Substitution

Raisins or chopped dried apricots work well if dates aren't available.

Storage Tip

Keep nuts fresh by storing them in the refrigerator or freezer until needed. They're rich in oil, which can become rancid at room temperature.

Prep Time: 10 minutes
(Ready in 35 minutes)

1½ cups whole wheat flour
½ cup cornmeal
½ cup chopped dates, if desired
⅓ cup sugar
¼ cup chopped nuts
1 teaspoon baking soda
½ teaspoon salt
1 cup buttermilk*
¼ cup molasses

1. Heat oven to 375°F. Grease bottoms only of 12 muffin cups. In medium bowl, combine flour, cornmeal, dates, sugar, nuts, baking soda and salt; mix well.
2. Add buttermilk and molasses; stir just until dry ingredients are moistened. Fill greased muffin cups about ¾ full.
3. Bake at 375°F. for 16 to 25 minutes or until toothpick inserted in center comes out clean. Cool 1 minute; remove from pan. Serve warm.

Yield: 12 muffins
High Altitude (Above 3,500 Feet): No change.

Tip: *To substitute for buttermilk, use 1 tablespoon vinegar or lemon juice plus milk to make 1 cup.

Nutrition Information Per Serving

Serving Size: 1 Muffin. Calories 160 • Calories from Fat 20 • Total Fat 2 g • Saturated Fat 0 g • Cholesterol 0 mg • Sodium 220 mg • Dietary Fiber 3 g
Dietary Exchanges: 1 Starch, 1 Fruit, ½ Fat OR 2 Carbohydrate, ½ Fat

---

Apricot Sunshine Muffins

Prep Time: 15 minutes
(Ready in 35 minutes)

1 cup all-purpose flour
1 cup whole wheat flour
1½ teaspoons baking soda
1 teaspoon grated orange peel
¼ teaspoon salt
1 (8-oz.) container low-fat
  apricot or orange yogurt

½ cup chopped dried apricots
⅓ cup orange juice
¼ cup honey
¼ cup oil
1 egg, slightly beaten

1. Heat oven to 375°F. Line 12 muffin cups with paper baking cups or grease bottoms only. In large bowl, combine all-purpose flour, whole wheat flour, baking soda, orange peel and salt; mix well.
2. In medium bowl, combine all remaining ingredients; mix well. Add to flour mixture; stir just until dry ingredients are moistened. Divide batter evenly into paper-lined muffin cups.
3. Bake at 375°F. for 14 to 18 minutes or until toothpick inserted in center comes out clean. Immediately remove from pan. Serve warm.

Yield: 12 muffins
High Altitude (Above 3,500 Feet): No change.

Nutrition Information Per Serving
Serving Size: 1 Muffin. Calories 180 • Calories from Fat 45 • Total Fat 5 g • Saturated Fat 1 g • Cholesterol 20 mg • Sodium 220 mg • Dietary Fiber 2 g Dietary Exchanges: 1 Starch, 1 Fruit, 1 Fat OR 2 Carbohydrate, 1 Fat

Kitchen Tip

There are two easy methods for removing the flavorful part of the citrus rind. One is grating with a fine-holed grater; the other is removing longer strips with a handheld "citrus zester," available in cookware shops. Be sure to remove only the colored part of the rind, which contains the flavorful essential oils; the white pith underneath is bitter.

Storage Tip

Because it includes bran, which contains oils, whole wheat flour is more perishable than all-purpose flour. Unless you bake with whole wheat flour frequently, store it in the refrigerator to maintain freshness.

gift idea

Golden Harvest Muffins

Menu Suggestion

The combination of shredded apples, coconut and raisins makes this muffin quite sweet. It's good with a slightly tangy spread such as crème fraîche or yogurt "cheese." To make yogurt cheese, set a coffee cone or funnel over a bowl and line it with a paper coffee filter. Fill the paper filter with plain nonfat yogurt and refrigerate it. After several hours, the liquid drips out into the bowl, leaving behind a thick, tangy, rich-tasting spread.

Storage Tip

Make and freeze a batch of these muffins. It takes just 30 seconds to warm one in the microwave for breakfast on the run.

Prep Time: 15 minutes
(Ready in 40 minutes)

1 cup all-purpose flour
1 cup whole wheat flour
1 cup sugar
2 teaspoons baking soda
2 teaspoons cinnamon
½ teaspoon salt
¼ teaspoon cloves
2 cups shredded peeled apples
½ cup shredded carrots

½ cup coconut
½ cup raisins
½ cup chopped walnuts or pecans
¾ cup oil
¼ cup milk
2 teaspoons vanilla
2 eggs, beaten

1. Heat oven to 350°F. Line 18 muffin cups with paper baking cups or grease muffin cups. In large bowl, combine all-purpose flour, whole wheat flour, sugar, baking soda, cinnamon, salt and cloves; mix well. Stir in apples, carrots, coconut, raisins and walnuts.
2. Add oil, milk, vanilla and eggs; stir just until dry ingredients are moistened. Fill paper-lined muffin cups ¾ full.
3. Bake at 350°F. for 20 to 25 minutes or until toothpick inserted in center comes out clean. Immediately remove from pan. Serve warm.

Yield: 18 muffins
High Altitude (Above 3,500 Feet): Increase all-purpose flour to 1¼ cups; decrease oil to ½ cup. Bake as directed above.

Nutrition Information Per Serving
Serving Size: 1 Muffin. Calories 250 • Calories from Fat 120 • Total Fat 13 g • Saturated Fat 2 g • Cholesterol 25 mg • Sodium 220 mg • Dietary Fiber 2 g
Dietary Exchanges: 1 Starch, 1 Fruit, 2½ Fat OR 2 Carbohydrate, 2½ Fat

Golden Harvest Muffins

Cranberry Upside-Down Muffins

• gift idea

Recipe Variation

Substitute 1 cup orange juice or buttermilk for the milk, and add ½ teaspoon baking soda to the dry ingredients.

Menu Suggestion

Pair the muffins with whipped cream cheese blended with orange marmalade or peach preserves.

Storage Tip

Cranberries make this a moist muffin that keeps better than most. Store leftovers in the refrigerator.

Prep Time: 15 minutes
(Ready in 35 minutes)

¾ cup whole berry cranberry sauce

¼ cup firmly packed brown sugar

2 cups all-purpose flour

2 tablespoons sugar

3 teaspoons baking powder

½ teaspoon salt

1 cup skim milk

¼ cup oil

1 teaspoon grated orange peel

2 egg whites

1. Heat oven to 400°F. Spray 12 muffin cups with non-stick cooking spray. Spoon 1 tablespoon cranberry sauce into each muffin cup; top each with 1 teaspoon brown sugar.

2. In large bowl, combine flour, sugar, baking powder and salt; mix well.

3. In small bowl, combine milk, oil, orange peel and egg whites; blend well. Add to flour mixture all at once; stir just until dry ingredients are moistened. Divide batter evenly over cranberries and brown sugar in muffin cups.

4. Bake at 400°F. for 14 to 18 minutes or until toothpick inserted in center comes out clean. Cool in pan 1 minute. Loosen muffin edges with knife; invert onto wire rack set over sheet of waxed paper. Cool 5 minutes. Serve warm.

Yield: 12 muffins
High Altitude (Above 3,500 Feet): No change.

Nutrition Information Per Serving
Serving Size: 1 Muffin. Calories 180 • Calories from Fat 45 • Total Fat 5 g •
Saturated Fat 1 g • Cholesterol 0 mg • Sodium 200 mg • Dietary Fiber 1 g
Dietary Exchanges: 1 Starch, 1 Fruit, 1 Fat OR 2 Carbohydrate, 1 Fat

Almond Streusel Mini-Muffins

Prep Time: 30 minutes

Topping

¼ cup sugar

¼ cup finely chopped blanched almonds

2 tablespoons all-purpose flour

2 tablespoons margarine or butter

Muffins

2 cups all-purpose flour

½ cup sugar

3 teaspoons baking powder

¼ teaspoon nutmeg

⅛ teaspoon salt

1 egg

¾ cup milk

⅓ cup oil

½ teaspoon almond extract

1. Heat oven to 400°F. Spray 36 miniature muffin cups with nonstick cooking spray. In small bowl, combine all topping ingredients; mix well. Set aside.

2. In medium bowl, combine 2 cups flour, ½ cup sugar, baking powder, nutmeg and salt; mix well. In another small bowl, beat egg slightly. Add milk, oil and almond extract; beat well. Add all at once to flour mixture; stir just until dry ingredients are moistened. Divide batter evenly into sprayed muffin cups. Sprinkle topping evenly over batter in cups.*

3. Bake at 400°F. for 10 to 15 minutes or until toothpick inserted in center comes out clean. Immediately remove from pan. Serve warm or cool.

Yield: 36 mini-muffins

High Altitude (Above 3,500 Feet): Decrease baking powder to 2 teaspoons. Bake as directed above.

Tip: *If necessary to bake muffins in batches, remaining batter can be held at room temperature for 30 minutes.

Nutrition Information Per Serving

Serving Size: 1 Mini-Muffin. Calories 70 • Calories from Fat 25 • Total Fat 3 g • Saturated Fat 1 g • Cholesterol 5 mg • Sodium 60 mg • Dietary Fiber 0 g Dietary Exchanges: ½ Starch, ½ Fat OR ½ Carbohydrate, ½ Fat

Recipe Fact

"Streusel" usually refers to a layer of spiced sugar, sometimes with nuts and other ingredients, sprinkled on top of a cake and often used to create a sweet filling in the middle of the cake.

Make It Special

For a Christmas party, bake the mini-muffins in tins lined with holiday-print cupcake papers.

Healthy Hint

To boost the protein and calcium content of any muffin recipe, stir in some dried milk powder along with the dry ingredients.

Lemon Poppy Seed Muffin Tops

Prep Time: 30 minutes

Muffin Tops
¾ cup all-purpose flour
¼ cup sugar
2 teaspoons baking powder
1 teaspoon poppy seed
¼ teaspoon salt
¼ teaspoon cinnamon
2 teaspoons grated lemon peel

3 tablespoons shortening
⅓ cup milk
1 teaspoon lemon juice

Topping
2 teaspoons sugar
Dash cinnamon

1. Heat oven to 400°F. In medium bowl, combine flour, ¼ cup sugar, baking powder, poppy seed, salt, ¼ teaspoon cinnamon and lemon peel; mix well. With pastry blender or fork, cut in shortening until mixture is crumbly.

2. Add milk and lemon juice; stir just until dry ingredients are moistened. Drop dough by tablespoonfuls onto ungreased cookie sheet.

3. In small bowl, combine topping ingredients; mix well. Sprinkle evenly over tops of dough.

4. Bake at 400°F. for 8 to 13 minutes or until light golden brown. Immediately remove from cookie sheet. Serve warm.

Yield: 9 muffin tops
High Altitude (Above 3,500 Feet): Increase flour to 1 cup;
decrease baking powder to 1½ teaspoons. Bake as directed above.

Nutrition Information Per Serving
Serving Size: 1 Muffin Top. Calories 110 • Calories from Fat 45 • Total Fat 5 g •
Saturated Fat 1 g • Cholesterol 0 mg • Sodium 170 mg • Dietary Fiber 0 g
Dietary Exchanges: ½ Starch, ½ Fruit, 1 Fat OR 1 Carbohydrate, 1 Fat

Recipe Fact

Just as kids prefer the frosted tops of cupcakes to the "plain" cake underneath, many adults think the sweetened top is the best part of muffins. This recipe caters to that view. By baking spoonfuls of batter on a cookie sheet instead of in muffin tins, the "muffin tops" resemble big, soft, sweet cookies.

Recipe Variation

Instead of making the muffins with poppy seed, stir 1 teaspoon caraway seed or ground cardamom into the batter.

Sweet Potato Muffins, page 43;
Lemon Poppy Seed Muffin Tops

Chocolate Chip Mini-Muffins

Prep Time: 30 minutes

low-fat   gift idea

Make It Special

Serve each guest a few mini-muffins on a saucer lined with a paper doily.

Ingredient Substitution

Make the muffins with miniature butterscotch chips.

Recipe Variation

Add ½ teaspoon ground cinnamon and a dash of ground nutmeg along with the dry ingredients.

Muffins
2 cups all-purpose flour
½ cup sugar
3 teaspoons baking powder
½ teaspoon salt
½ cup miniature chocolate chips

1 egg
¾ cup skim milk
¼ cup oil

Topping
3 tablespoons sugar
2 tablespoons brown sugar

1. Heat oven to 400°F. Spray 36 miniature muffin cups with nonstick cooking spray. In large bowl, combine flour, ½ cup sugar, baking powder, salt and chocolate chips; mix well.
2. In small bowl, beat egg. Stir in milk and oil. Add to flour mixture; stir just until dry ingredients are moistened. (Batter will be lumpy.) Divide batter evenly into sprayed muffin cups, filling each ¾ full.*
3. In small bowl, combine topping ingredients; mix well. Sprinkle evenly over batter in cups.
4. Bake at 400°F. for 10 to 15 minutes or until golden brown. Immediately run knife around sides of muffin cups to loosen muffins; remove muffins from pan. Serve warm.

Yield: 36 mini-muffins
High Altitude (Above 3,500 Feet): No change.

Tip: *If necessary to bake muffins in batches, remaining batter can be held at room temperature for 30 minutes.

Nutrition Information Per Serving
Serving Size: 1 Mini-Muffin. Calories 70 • Calories from Fat 20 • Total Fat 2 g • Saturated Fat 1 g • Cholesterol 5 mg • Sodium 75 mg • Dietary Fiber 0 g
Dietary Exchanges: ½ Fruit, ½ Fat OR ½ Carbohydrate, ½ Fat

Strawberry Mini-Muffins

Prep Time: 15 minutes
(Ready in 35 minutes)

2 cups all-purpose flour	$\frac{1}{3}$ cup oil
$\frac{1}{2}$ cup sugar	1 egg
3 teaspoons baking powder	1 cup chopped fresh
$\frac{1}{2}$ teaspoon salt	strawberries
$\frac{3}{4}$ cup milk	2 tablespoons sugar

1. Heat oven to 375°F. Spray 36 miniature muffin cups with nonstick cooking spray. In large bowl, combine flour, $\frac{1}{2}$ cup sugar, baking powder and salt; mix well.
2. In small bowl, combine milk, oil and egg; blend well. Add to flour mixture; stir just until dry ingredients are moistened. Gently stir in strawberries. Spoon rounded tablespoonful batter into each sprayed muffin cup. Sprinkle 2 tablespoons sugar evenly over batter in cups.*
3. Bake at 375°F. for 12 to 16 minutes or until edges are very light golden brown and toothpick inserted in center comes out clean. Cool 3 minutes; remove from pan. Serve warm.

Yield: 36 mini-muffins
High Altitude (Above 3,500 Feet): No change.

Tip: *If necessary to bake muffins in batches, remaining batter can be refrigerated and baked as soon as possible.

Nutrition Information Per Serving
Serving Size: 1 Mini-Muffin. Calories 60 • Calories from Fat 20 • Total Fat 2 g •
Saturated Fat 0 g • Cholesterol 5 mg • Sodium 75 mg • Dietary Fiber 0 g
Dietary Exchanges: $\frac{1}{2}$ Starch, $\frac{1}{2}$ Fat OR $\frac{1}{2}$ Carbohydrate, $\frac{1}{2}$ Fat

---

About Strawberries

Purchase fresh strawberries that are dark red and without white tips or signs of mold or mushiness. Use them within a day or so of purchase. Rinse berries, then remove their green hulls. Doing the reverse can waterlog the berries.

Make It Special

For a strawberry shortcake variation, split these muffins, then fill and top them with additional (uncooked) sliced fresh berries and mounds of real whipped cream.

Ingredient Substitution

Substitute raspberries or chopped ripe peaches for the strawberries.

Banana Mini-Muffins

Prep Time: 30 minutes

1 cup all-purpose flour
1 cup whole wheat flour
½ cup sugar
2 teaspoons baking powder
½ teaspoon baking soda
½ teaspoon nutmeg
⅛ teaspoon salt

⅛ teaspoon allspice
1 egg
½ cup buttermilk*
½ cup (1 medium) mashed ripe
   banana
⅓ cup oil

About Buttermilk

Originally, buttermilk was the liquid left after butter was churned. Today, it's made commercially by adding special bacteria cultures to low-fat or nonfat milk. Despite buttermilk's thick consistency and rich flavor, it is a low-fat or nonfat product. In baking, it provides tang and tenderness.

Recipe Variation

Stir ½ cup finely chopped walnuts into the batter.

Make It Special

Dress up the muffins with a drizzle of icing made with powdered sugar and lemon juice.

1. Heat oven to 400°F. Spray 36 miniature muffin cups with nonstick cooking spray or line with paper baking cups. In large bowl, combine all-purpose flour, whole wheat flour, sugar, baking powder, baking soda, nutmeg, salt and allspice; mix well.

2. In small bowl, beat egg. Add buttermilk, banana and oil; mix well. Add to flour mixture; stir just until dry ingredients are moistened. Divide batter evenly into sprayed muffin cups, filling each ⅔ full.**

3. Bake at 400°F. for 10 to 15 minutes or until muffins are light golden brown and toothpick inserted in center comes out clean. Immediately remove from pan. Serve warm.

Yield: 36 mini-muffins
High Altitude (Above 3,500 Feet): Decrease sugar to ¼ cup. Bake as directed above.

Tips: *To substitute for buttermilk, use 1½ teaspoons vinegar or lemon juice plus milk to make ½ cup.

**If necessary to bake muffins in batches, remaining batter can be refrigerated and baked as soon as possible.

Nutrition Information Per Serving
Serving Size: 1 Mini-Muffin. Calories 60 • Calories from Fat 20 • Total Fat 2 g • Saturated Fat 0 g • Cholesterol 5 mg • Sodium 60 mg • Dietary Fiber 1 g Dietary Exchanges: ½ Starch, ½ Fat OR ½ Carbohydrate, ½ Fat

Banana Mini-Muffins; Strawberry Mini-Muffins, page 55

Banana-Blueberry Streusel Muffins

About Blueberries

In the supermarket, you're most likely to find large, cultivated blueberries. Wild blueberries are much smaller and often more flavorful. Store blueberries loosely covered in the refrigerator, and use them within a day or two. Pick through fresh blueberries to remove any stems or wilted berries before rinsing and draining thoroughly.

Storage Tip

When blueberries are abundant and inexpensive, stock up and freeze them. Arrange berries in a single layer on a baking tray and freeze them. When they're frozen, pop them into a resealable plastic freezer bag or container so you'll be able to pour out the amount needed at a later date.

Prep Time: 20 minutes
(Ready in 50 minutes)

Muffins
$\frac{1}{2}$ cup margarine, softened
$\frac{1}{2}$ cup packed brown sugar
$1\frac{1}{2}$ cups (3 medium) mashed
   very ripe bananas
$\frac{1}{4}$ cup milk
1 teaspoon vanilla
2 eggs
2 cups all-purpose flour
1 teaspoon baking powder
1 teaspoon baking soda
$\frac{1}{4}$ teaspoon salt
1 cup fresh or frozen
   blueberries (do not thaw)

Streusel Topping
3 tablespoons all-purpose flour
2 tablespoons firmly packed
   brown sugar
$\frac{1}{2}$ teaspoon cinnamon
2 tablespoons margarine
$\frac{1}{4}$ cup chopped walnuts

1. Heat oven to 375°F. Grease bottoms only of 18 muffin cups or line with paper baking cups. In large bowl, combine $\frac{1}{2}$ cup margarine and $\frac{1}{2}$ cup brown sugar; beat until fluffy. Add bananas, milk, vanilla and eggs; blend well.
2. Add 2 cups flour, baking powder, baking soda and salt; stir just until dry ingredients are moistened. Gently stir in blueberries. Fill greased muffin cups $\frac{3}{4}$ full.
3. In small bowl, combine 3 tablespoons flour, 2 tablespoons brown sugar and cinnamon; mix well. With pastry blender or fork, cut in 2 tablespoons margarine until mixture is crumbly. Stir in walnuts. Sprinkle over batter.
4. Bake at 375°F. for 18 to 23 minutes or until toothpick inserted in center comes out clean. Cool 3 minutes; remove from pan. Serve warm.

Yield: 18 muffins
High Altitude (Above 3,500 Feet): No change.

Nutrition Information Per Serving
Serving Size: 1 Muffin. Calories 200 • Calories from Fat 80 • Total Fat 9 g •
Saturated Fat 2 g • Cholesterol 25 mg • Sodium 210 mg • Dietary Fiber 1 g
Dietary Exchanges: 1 Starch, 1 Fruit, $1\frac{1}{2}$ Fat OR 2 Carbohydrate, $1\frac{1}{2}$ Fat

Streusel-Topped Pumpkin Muffins

Prep Time: 15 minutes
(Ready in 40 minutes)

Streusel Topping
2 tablespoons brown sugar
2 tablespoons finely chopped
  nuts
1 tablespoon all-purpose flour
$\frac{1}{4}$ teaspoon cinnamon
1 tablespoon margarine or
  butter, softened

Muffins
1 egg, beaten
$\frac{1}{2}$ cup milk

$\frac{1}{2}$ cup canned pumpkin
$\frac{1}{3}$ cup oil
$1\frac{3}{4}$ cups all-purpose flour
$\frac{1}{2}$ cup sugar
3 teaspoons baking powder
$\frac{1}{2}$ teaspoon salt
$\frac{1}{2}$ teaspoon cinnamon
$\frac{1}{2}$ teaspoon nutmeg
$\frac{1}{4}$ teaspoon cloves
$\frac{1}{4}$ cup chopped nuts
$\frac{1}{4}$ cup raisins

editor's favorite • gift idea

Kitchen Tip
To freshen up leftover muffins, reheat them briefly in the microwave or conventional oven.

Make It Special
As a gift for a new or expert baker, pair up a batch of these muffins with a copy of this book and a special bookmark indicating the recipe.

1. Heat oven to 400°F. Line 12 muffin cups with paper baking cups or grease bottoms only. In small bowl, combine all topping ingredients; mix until crumbly. Set aside.
2. In medium bowl, combine egg, milk, pumpkin and oil; blend well. Add $1\frac{3}{4}$ cups flour, sugar, baking powder, salt, $\frac{1}{2}$ teaspoon cinnamon, nutmeg and cloves; stir just until dry ingredients are moistened. (Batter will be lumpy.) Stir in $\frac{1}{4}$ cup nuts and raisins. Fill paper-lined muffin cups $\frac{2}{3}$ full. Sprinkle streusel evenly over batter in cups.
3. Bake at 400°F. for 18 to 22 minutes or until toothpick inserted in center comes out clean. Immediately remove from pan. Serve warm.

Yield: 12 muffins
High Altitude (Above 3,500 Feet): No change.

Nutrition Information Per Serving
Serving Size: 1 Muffin. Calories 230 • Calories from Fat 90 • Total Fat 10 g •
Saturated Fat 1 g • Cholesterol 20 mg • Sodium 230 mg • Dietary Fiber 1 g
Dietary Exchanges: 1 Starch, 1 Fruit, 2 Fat OR 2 Carbohydrate, 2 Fat

Peach Streusel Muffins

Prep Time: 20 minutes
(Ready in 35 minutes)

Make It Special

For a nice gourmet-shop type of gift, package a few "sampler"-sized packs of flavored coffee, a batch of these muffins and miniature jars of jam.

Recipe Variation

Quadruple the topping and use it for baked apple or peach crisp.

Storage Tip

These muffins freeze well for up to three months. Place cooled muffins in a tightly covered tin or plastic container, or arrange them in a single layer in a resealable plastic freezer bag.

Streusel Topping
- ¼ cup rolled oats
- 1 tablespoon chopped pecans
- 1 tablespoon shreds of whole bran cereal
- 2 tablespoons brown sugar
- 2 teaspoons margarine, melted
- ⅓ cup packed brown sugar
- 3 tablespoons margarine
- 1 egg
- 1½ cups all-purpose flour
- ¼ cup rolled oats
- 2 teaspoons baking powder
- ½ teaspoon baking soda
- ¼ teaspoon salt
- ¼ teaspoon nutmeg
- ½ teaspoon vanilla

Muffins
- Milk
- 1 (8.75-oz.) can peach slices, drained, reserving liquid

1. Heat oven to 375°F. Line 12 muffin cups with paper baking cups and spray paper cups with nonstick cooking spray. In small bowl, combine all topping ingredients; mix well. Set aside.

2. Add milk to reserved peach liquid to make ½ cup. In blender container or food processor bowl with metal blade, process peach slices until smooth.

3. In large bowl, combine ⅓ cup brown sugar and 3 tablespoons margarine; beat until well blended. Add milk mixture, peaches and egg; blend well. Add all remaining muffin ingredients; stir just until combined. Divide batter evenly into paper-lined muffin cups. Sprinkle about 2 teaspoons topping onto batter in each cup.

4. Bake at 375°F. for 10 to 15 minutes or until light golden brown. Immediately remove from pan. Serve warm.

Yield: 12 muffins
High Altitude (Above 3,500 Feet): Increase flour to 1⅔ cups. Bake as directed above.

Nutrition Information Per Serving
Serving Size: 1 Muffin. Calories 170 • Calories from Fat 50 • Total Fat 6 g •
Saturated Fat 1 g • Cholesterol 20 mg • Sodium 250 mg • Dietary Fiber 1 g
Dietary Exchanges: 1 Starch, 1 Fruit, 1 Fat OR 2 Carbohydrate, 1 Fat

Graham Streusel Lemon Muffins

Prep Time: 20 minutes
(Ready in 40 minutes)

Streusel Topping

3 tablespoons graham cracker
  crumbs
2 tablespoons brown sugar
1 tablespoon margarine or
  butter, softened

Muffins

1½ cups all-purpose flour
½ cup sugar
2 teaspoons baking powder
½ teaspoon baking soda
¼ teaspoon salt
1 (8-oz.) container low-fat
  lemon yogurt
2 tablespoons oil
1 tablespoon grated lemon
  peel
1 egg

1. Heat oven to 400°F. Line 10 muffin cups with paper baking cups and spray paper cups with nonstick cooking spray. In small bowl, combine all topping ingredients; mix well. Set aside.
2. In medium bowl, combine flour, sugar, baking powder, baking soda and salt; mix well.
3. In another small bowl, combine yogurt, oil, lemon peel and egg; beat well. Add to flour mixture; stir just until dry ingredients are moistened. (Batter will be stiff.) Divide batter evenly into sprayed paper-lined muffin cups. Sprinkle streusel evenly over batter in cups.
4. Bake at 400°F. for 12 to 18 minutes or until toothpick inserted in center comes out clean. Immediately remove from pan. Serve warm.

Yield: 10 muffins
High Altitude (Above 3,500 Feet): No change.

Nutrition Information Per Serving

Serving Size: 1 Muffin. Calories 180 • Calories from Fat 45 • Total Fat 5 g •
Saturated Fat 1 g • Cholesterol 25 mg • Sodium 260 mg • Dietary Fiber 1 g
Dietary Exchanges: 1 Starch, 1 Fruit, 1 Fat OR 2 Carbohydrate, 1 Fat

---

Kitchen Tip

When purchasing low-fat flavored yogurt for baking, be sure to buy the kind made with regular sugar, not sweetened with aspartame.

Make It Special

For a theme gift, package a batch of Graham Streusel Lemon Muffins in a basket lined with a yellow kitchen towel. Add a box of lemon-flavored tea and yellow cocktail napkins.

Recipe Variation

To make Lemon Poppy Seed Muffins, a popular flavor combination, stir 1½ teaspoons poppy seed into the batter.

Graham Nut Muffins

Prep Time: 15 minutes
(Ready in 35 minutes)

1 cup graham cracker crumbs
(about 12 crackers)
½ cup all-purpose flour
¼ cup whole wheat flour
½ cup firmly packed brown
sugar
3 teaspoons baking powder

¼ cup chopped pecans, if
desired
¼ cup chopped dates
3 egg whites
½ cup skim milk
¼ cup oil

1. Heat oven to 375°F. Line 12 muffin cups with paper baking cups or generously grease. In large bowl, combine graham cracker crumbs, all-purpose flour, whole wheat flour, brown sugar and baking powder; mix well. Stir in pecans and dates.

2. In small bowl, slightly beat egg whites. Add milk and oil; blend well. Add to flour mixture all at once; stir just until dry ingredients are moistened. Fill paper-lined muffin cups ¾ full.

3. Bake at 375°F. for 16 to 19 minutes or until toothpick inserted in center comes out clean. Cool 1 minute; remove from pan. Serve warm.

Yield: 12 muffins
High Altitude (Above 3,500 Feet): Increase all-purpose flour to ¾ cup.
Bake as directed above.

Nutrition Information Per Serving
Serving Size: 1 Muffin. Calories 170 • Calories from Fat 60 • Total Fat 7 g •
Saturated Fat 1 g • Cholesterol 0 mg • Sodium 190 mg • Dietary Fiber 1 g
Dietary Exchanges: 1 Starch, ½ Fruit, 1½ Fat OR 1½ Carbohydrate, 1½ Fat

About Pecans

Pecans, which grow in the American Southeast, have nutmeats that are similar in shape to walnuts but are flatter and have a slightly softer texture and sweeter flavor.

Kitchen Tip

To make graham cracker crumbs, seal the crackers inside a resealable plastic bag, squeezing out all the air, then crush them with a rolling pin.

Make It Special

For a community bake sale, wrap cooled muffins individually and tie each with a ribbon.

Graham Nut Muffins

Banana Oat Muffins

Ingredient Substitution

For muffins with more texture, use old-fashioned rolled oats instead of quick-cooking oats.

Healthy Hint

When bananas start looking speckled and even doubling this muffin recipe won't use up all of the rapidly ripening fruit, freeze banana slices in a single layer on a baking sheet or cut each banana into two pieces and insert a wooden stick "handle" into the cut end of each and freeze. Frozen bananas develop a wonderful texture and sweet flavor for a delicious, healthful snack.

Storage Tip

Bananas and buttermilk both contribute moisture that helps these muffins maintain freshness longer than some others. Even so, they should be stored in a tightly covered container or on a plate wrapped in plastic. If they seem dry, reheat the muffins briefly in the microwave oven.

Prep Time: 15 minutes
(Ready in 35 minutes)

Muffins

1¼ cups all-purpose flour
½ cup quick-cooking rolled oats
¼ cup sugar
2½ teaspoons baking powder
½ teaspoon cinnamon
¼ teaspoon nutmeg
1 cup (2 medium) mashed ripe bananas
½ cup buttermilk*
3 tablespoons oil
1 egg

Topping

1 tablespoon sugar
⅛ teaspoon cinnamon

1. Heat oven to 400°F. Spray bottoms only of 12 muffin cups with nonstick cooking spray. In large bowl, combine flour, oats, ¼ cup sugar, baking powder, ½ teaspoon cinnamon and nutmeg; mix well.
2. In small bowl, combine bananas, buttermilk, oil and egg; beat well. Add to flour mixture; stir just until dry ingredients are moistened. Fill sprayed muffin cups ¾ full.
3. In another small bowl, combine topping ingredients; mix well. Sprinkle evenly over batter in cups.
4. Bake at 400°F. for 15 to 18 minutes or until toothpick inserted in center comes out clean. Cool 1 minute; remove from pan. Serve warm.

Yield: 12 muffins
High Altitude (Above 3,500 Feet): Increase flour to 1⅓ cups; decrease baking powder to 2 teaspoons. Bake as directed above.

Tip: *To substitute for buttermilk, use 1½ teaspoons vinegar or lemon juice plus milk to make ½ cup.

Nutrition Information Per Serving

Serving Size: 1 Muffin. Calories 140 • Calories from Fat 35 • Total Fat 4 g • Saturated Fat 1 g • Cholesterol 20 mg • Sodium 120 mg • Dietary Fiber 1 g Dietary Exchanges: 1 Starch, ½ Fruit, ½ Fat OR 1½ Carbohydrate, ½ Fat

Oats 'n Wheat Blueberry Muffins

fiber source

Prep Time: 20 minutes
(Ready in 45 minutes)

1 cup quick-cooking rolled oats
1¼ cups buttermilk*
½ cup honey
¼ cup oil
1 egg, slightly beaten

1½ cups whole wheat flour
1 teaspoon baking soda
½ teaspoon salt
1 cup fresh or frozen
   blueberries (do not thaw)

1. In large bowl, combine rolled oats and buttermilk; mix well. Let stand 5 minutes. Heat oven to 375°F. Grease 12 muffin cups or line with paper baking cups.
2. Add honey, oil and egg to oats mixture; blend well. In small bowl, combine flour, baking soda and salt; mix well. Add to oats mixture; stir just until dry ingredients are moistened. Gently stir in blueberries. Fill greased muffin cups about ¾ full.
3. Bake at 375°F. for 20 to 25 minutes or until toothpick inserted in center comes out clean. Immediately remove from pan. Serve warm.

Yield: 12 muffins
High Altitude (Above 3,500 Feet): Increase flour to 1¾ cups.
Divide batter evenly into 15 muffin cups. Bake as directed above.

Tip: *To substitute for buttermilk, use 3¾ teaspoons vinegar or lemon juice plus milk to make 1¼ cups.

Nutrition Information Per Serving

Serving Size: 1 Muffin. Calories 190 • Calories from Fat 50 • Total Fat 6 g •
Saturated Fat 1 g • Cholesterol 20 mg • Sodium 230 mg • Dietary Fiber 3 g
Dietary Exchanges: 1½ Starch, ½ Fruit, 1 Fat OR 2 Carbohydrate, 1 Fat

---

Recipe Variation

Substitute 1 cup chopped fresh or frozen cranberries for the blueberries.

Menu Suggestion

Serve these with coffee for breakfast or as a refreshingly different accompaniment to fruited chicken salad at lunch.

Orange Oat Bran Muffins

Prep Time: 20 minutes
(Ready in 40 minutes)

Make It Special

As a housewarming gift for a young person just striking out on his or her own, present the muffins in a new muffin tin along with the recipe and a package of muffin paper liners.

Ingredient Substitution

Oat bran lends flavor and heartiness to the batter, but if you prefer more texture, substitute rolled oats.

Recipe Variation

Make the muffins with ½ cup chopped dried apricots or dried cherries instead of raisins.

1 cup oat bran hot cereal, uncooked
½ cup firmly packed brown sugar
¾ cup skim milk
¼ cup orange juice
1 cup whole wheat flour
2 teaspoons baking powder
1 teaspoon cinnamon
1 teaspoon grated orange peel
½ teaspoon salt
½ cup refrigerated or frozen fat-free egg product, thawed, or 2 eggs, slightly beaten
⅓ cup oil
½ cup raisins

1. Heat oven to 400°F. Line 12 muffin cups with paper baking cups or grease. In medium bowl, combine cereal, brown sugar, milk and orange juice; mix well. Let stand 10 minutes.

2. Add all remaining ingredients; stir just until dry ingredients are moistened. Fill paper-lined muffin cups ¾ full.

3. Bake at 400°F. for 15 to 18 minutes or until toothpick inserted in center comes out clean. Immediately remove from pan. Serve warm.

Yield: 12 muffins

High Altitude (Above 3,500 Feet): Increase flour to 1 cup plus 2 tablespoons. Bake as directed above.

Nutrition Information Per Serving

Serving Size: 1 Muffin. Calories 160 • Calories from Fat 50 • Total Fat 6 g • Saturated Fat 1 g • Cholesterol 0 mg • Sodium 200 mg • Dietary Fiber 1 g Dietary Exchanges: 1 Starch, ½ Fruit, 1 Fat OR 1½ Carbohydrate, 1 Fat

Whole Wheat Apple Muffins

Prep Time: 20 minutes
(Ready in 45 minutes)

Muffins

1½ cups all-purpose flour
1½ cups chopped peeled
  apples
½ cup whole wheat flour
½ cup packed brown sugar
2 teaspoons baking powder
¼ teaspoon salt
¼ teaspoon cinnamon
½ cup skim milk
¼ cup margarine or butter,
  melted

¼ cup refrigerated or frozen
  fat-free egg product,
  thawed, or 1 egg, slightly
  beaten

Topping

¼ cup packed brown sugar
1 tablespoon finely chopped
  nuts
¼ teaspoon cinnamon

1. Heat oven to 400°F. Grease bottoms only of 12 muffin cups or line with paper baking cups. In small bowl, combine ½ cup of the all-purpose flour and apples; stir until apples are well coated.
2. In large bowl, combine remaining 1 cup all-purpose flour, whole wheat flour, ½ cup brown sugar, baking powder, salt and ¼ teaspoon cinnamon; mix well. Add apples and all remaining muffin ingredients; stir just until dry ingredients are moistened. Divide batter evenly into greased muffin cups.
3. In small bowl, combine all topping ingredients; sprinkle about 2 teaspoons over each cup.
4. Bake at 400°F. for 20 to 25 minutes or until toothpick inserted in center comes out clean. Immediately remove from pan. Serve warm.

Yield: 12 muffins
High Altitude (Above 3,500 Feet): No change.

Nutrition Information Per Serving

Serving Size: 1 Muffin. Calories 190 • Calories from Fat 45 • Total Fat 5 g •
Saturated Fat 1 g • Cholesterol 0 mg • Sodium 190 mg • Dietary Fiber 1 g
Dietary Exchanges: 1 Starch, 1 Fruit, 1 Fat OR 2 Carbohydrate, 1 Fat

Kitchen Tip

Are some of yesterday's muffins left? Use them to make an impromptu "trifle" dessert. Fold chunks of muffin into vanilla pudding and top with a spoonful of whipped cream.

Make It Special

Pipe a spiral design on the top of each muffin with a glaze made of powdered sugar mixed with milk and a few drops of pure vanilla extract.

Ingredient Substitution

Try the recipe with chopped pear instead of apple.

Refrigerator Apple Bran Muffins

Ingredient Substitution

To substitute for butter-milk, use 1 tablespoon plus 1½ teaspoons vinegar or lemon juice plus milk to make 1½ cups.

Kitchen Tip

To separate eggs easily, crack eggs into a funnel held over a mug or bowl. The white will slip through the neck of the funnel into the mug; the yolk will remain in the mouth of the funnel, ready to be poured into another bowl. Egg yolks can be used to make custard or custard-based ice cream.

Prep Time: 15 minutes
(Ready in 35 minutes)

2 cups shreds of whole bran cereal
1½ cups buttermilk
2 cups all-purpose flour
½ cup whole wheat flour
1 cup sugar
1 teaspoon baking powder
1 teaspoon baking soda

1 teaspoon cinnamon
1 teaspoon ginger
¼ teaspoon salt
½ cup raisins
1 cup unsweetened applesauce
½ cup oil
4 egg whites

1. In medium bowl, combine cereal and buttermilk; mix well. Let stand 5 minutes until cereal is softened.
2. Meanwhile, in large bowl, combine all-purpose flour, whole wheat flour, sugar, baking powder, baking soda, cinnamon, ginger, salt and raisins; mix well.
3. To cereal mixture, add applesauce, oil and egg whites; blend well. Add to flour mixture all at once; stir just until dry ingredients are moistened. Batter can be baked immediately or stored in tightly covered container in refrigerator for up to 2 weeks.
4. When ready to bake, heat oven to 400° F. Spray desired number of muffin cups with nonstick cooking spray or line with paper baking cups. Stir batter; fill sprayed muffin cups ¾ full.
5. Bake at 400° F. for 15 to 20 minutes or until toothpick inserted in center comes out clean. Serve warm.

Yield: 30 muffins
High Altitude (Above 3,500 Feet): Increase all-purpose flour to 2¼ cups.
Bake as directed above.

Refrigerator Apple Bran Muffins

Nutrition Information Per Serving
Serving Size: 1 Muffin. Calories 130 • Calories from Fat 35 • Total Fat 4 g • Saturated Fat 1 g • Cholesterol 0 mg • Sodium 105 mg • Dietary Fiber 2 g
Dietary Exchanges: 1 Starch, ½ Fruit, ½ Fat OR 1½ Carbohydrate, ½ Fat

Banana Snack Muffins

Ingredient Substitution

One cup of plain nonfat yogurt and 1 teaspoon of vanilla or 1 cup of apple-sauce may be used in place of the vanilla yogurt.

Kitchen Tip

If you're mincing a small amount of nuts, such as for the topping of the Banana Snack Muffins, use a large chef's knife and a cutting board or an old-fashioned manual nut chopper and a wooden bowl. For larger quanti-ties, use a food processor or a blender, but be sure to process with on/off pulses to prevent the nuts from turning into nut butter.

Make It Special

Sprinkle the top of each muffin with miniature chocolate chips before baking.

Muffins
¾ cup all-purpose flour
½ cup whole wheat flour
1½ teaspoons baking powder
¼ teaspoon salt
½ cup sugar
3 tablespoons margarine or butter, softened
¾ cup (about 1 large) mashed ripe banana
1 (8-oz.) container low-fat vanilla yogurt
2 egg whites

Topping
1 tablespoon sugar
2 teaspoons finely chopped walnuts
¼ teaspoon nutmeg

1. Heat oven to 375°F. Spray bottoms only of 12 muffin cups with nonstick cooking spray. In large bowl, combine all-purpose flour, whole wheat flour, baking powder and salt; mix well.

2. In medium bowl, combine ½ cup sugar and mar-garine; beat at low speed until well blended. Add banana, yogurt and egg whites; beat well. Add to flour mixture; stir with spoon just until dry ingredients are moistened. Divide batter evenly into sprayed muffin cups.

3. In small bowl, combine all topping ingredients; mix well. Sprinkle evenly over batter in cups.

4. Bake at 375°F. for 20 to 25 minutes or until toothpick inserted in center comes out clean. Immediately remove from pan; cool slightly. Serve warm.

Yield: 12 muffins
High Altitude (Above 3,500 Feet): Increase all-purpose flour to 1 cup.
Bake as directed above.

Nutrition Information Per Serving
Serving Size: 1 Muffin. Calories 150 • Calories from Fat 35 • Total Fat 4 g •
Saturated Fat 1 g • Cholesterol 0 mg • Sodium 160 mg • Dietary Fiber 1 g
Dietary Exchanges: 1½ Starch, ½ Fat OR 1½ Carbohydrate, ½ Fat

Whole Wheat Banana Muffins

Prep Time: 15 minutes
(Ready in 45 minutes)

⅓ cup margarine or butter, softened
½ cup firmly packed brown sugar
1½ cups (3 medium) mashed ripe bananas
½ cup refrigerated or frozen fat-free egg product, thawed, or 2 eggs
¼ cup skim milk
1 teaspoon vanilla
¾ cup all-purpose flour
¾ cup whole wheat flour
½ cup wheat germ
1 teaspoon baking powder
1 teaspoon baking soda
3 tablespoons chopped walnuts

1. Heat oven to 375°F. Grease 18 muffin cups. In large bowl, combine margarine and brown sugar; beat until fluffy. Add bananas, egg product, milk and vanilla; blend well.
2. Add all-purpose flour, whole wheat flour, wheat germ, baking powder and baking soda; stir just until dry ingredients are moistened. Fill greased muffin cups ⅔ full. Sprinkle walnuts evenly over batter in cups.
3. Bake at 375°F. for 20 to 25 minutes or until toothpick inserted in center comes out clean. Cool 5 minutes; remove from pan. Serve warm.

Yield: 18 muffins
High Altitude (Above 3,500 Feet): Increase all-purpose flour to 1 cup.
Bake as directed above.

Nutrition Information Per Serving

Serving Size: 1 Muffin. Calories 140 • Calories from Fat 45 • Total Fat 5 g •
Saturated Fat 1 g • Cholesterol 0 mg • Sodium 150 mg • Dietary Fiber 2 g
Dietary Exchanges: 1 Starch, ½ Fruit, 1 Fat OR 1½ Carbohydrate, 1 Fat

Kitchen Tip

Although a fork will work, a hand-held potato masher or potato ricer makes short work of mashing bananas. The best bananas for baking have at least some brown speckles on the skin.

Storage Tip

Wheat germ has a high oil content. Store it in the refrigerator to prevent spoiling.

Dried Blueberry Whole Wheat Muffins

Prep Time: 30 minutes

1 cup all-purpose flour
¾ cup whole wheat flour
½ cup firmly packed brown sugar
2 teaspoons baking powder
½ teaspoon baking soda
½ teaspoon salt

1 cup buttermilk*
¼ cup oil
2 egg whites
½ cup dried blueberries, dried tart cherries, sweetened dried cranberries or raisins

1. Heat oven to 400°F. Spray 12 muffin cups with nonstick cooking spray, or line muffin cups with paper baking cups and spray paper cups with nonstick cooking spray.

2. In large bowl, combine all-purpose flour, whole wheat flour, brown sugar, baking powder, baking soda and salt; mix well.

3. In small bowl, combine buttermilk, oil and egg whites; blend well. Add to flour mixture all at once; stir just until dry ingredients are moistened. Gently stir in dried blueberries. Spoon batter evenly into sprayed muffin cups.

4. Bake at 400°F. for 14 to 19 minutes or until muffins are light golden brown and toothpick inserted in center comes out clean. Immediately remove from pan. Serve warm.

Yield: 12 muffins
High Altitude (Above 3,500 Feet): Increase all-purpose flour to 1¼ cups.
Bake at 400°F. for 17 to 21 minutes.

Tip: *To substitute for buttermilk, use 1 tablespoon vinegar or lemon juice plus milk to make 1 cup.

Nutrition Information Per Serving
Serving Size: 1 Muffin. Calories 180 • Calories from Fat 45 • Total Fat 5 g •
Saturated Fat 1 g • Cholesterol 0 mg • Sodium 260 mg • Dietary Fiber 2 g
Dietary Exchanges: 1 Starch, 1 Fruit, 1 Fat OR 2 Carbohydrate, 1 Fat

Whole Wheat Maple Muffins

Prep Time: 15 minutes
(Ready in 40 minutes)

editor's favorite • fiber source

Make It Special

Press a walnut half into the glaze on top of each muffin.

Menu Suggestion

Serve these muffins with an omelet and bacon as part of a hearty breakfast.

Muffins

1½ cups whole wheat flour
½ cup firmly packed brown sugar
2 teaspoons baking powder
½ teaspoon salt
1 egg
½ cup skim milk
½ cup unsweetened applesauce
¼ cup oil
2 tablespoons maple flavor
½ cup chopped dates

Glaze

¼ cup powdered sugar
1 teaspoon maple flavor
¼ to ½ teaspoon skim milk

1. Heat oven to 375°F. Line 12 muffin cups with paper baking cups or spray with nonstick cooking spray. In large bowl, combine flour, brown sugar, baking powder and salt; mix well.

2. In small bowl, beat egg until foamy. Add ½ cup milk, applesauce, oil and 2 tablespoons maple flavor; blend well. Add to flour mixture; stir just until dry ingredients are moistened. Stir in dates. Fill paper-lined muffin cups ¾ full.

3. Bake at 375°F. for 19 to 22 minutes or until toothpick inserted in center comes out clean. Immediately remove from pan.

4. In small bowl, blend all glaze ingredients, adding enough milk for desired drizzling consistency. Drizzle over warm muffins. Serve warm.

Yield: 12 muffins
High Altitude (Above 3,500 Feet): No change.

Nutrition Information Per Serving

Serving Size: 1 Muffin. Calories 180 • Calories from Fat 45 • Total Fat 5 g •
Saturated Fat 1 g • Cholesterol 20 mg • Sodium 190 mg • Dietary Fiber 3 g
Dietary Exchanges: 1 Starch, 1 Fruit, 1 Fat OR 2 Carbohydrate, 1 Fat

Make It Special

Peanut butter and jelly spread on a muffin instead of ordinary bread is a nice lunchbox surprise for kids.

Menu Suggestion

Serve the muffins with fresh-squeezed orange juice, coffee or tea and your favorite omelet.

Fruity Orange Refrigerator Muffins

Prep Time: 15 minutes
(Ready in 3 hours 35 minutes)

1½ cups all-purpose flour
1 cup whole wheat flour
2 cups shreds of whole bran cereal
1½ cups sugar
1¼ teaspoons baking soda
1 teaspoon baking powder
½ teaspoon salt

¼ teaspoon allspice
1 tablespoon grated orange peel
2½ cups buttermilk*
½ cup oil
2 eggs, slightly beaten
1 (6-oz.) pkg. dried fruit bits

1. In large bowl, combine all-purpose flour, whole wheat flour, cereal, sugar, baking soda, baking powder, salt, allspice and orange peel; mix well. Add buttermilk, oil and eggs; mix well. Stir in fruit bits. Cover tightly; refrigerate at least 3 hours or up to 2 weeks.

2. When ready to bake, heat oven to 400°F. Grease desired number of muffin cups or line with paper baking cups. Stir batter; fill greased muffin cups ¾ full.

3. Bake at 400°F. for 18 to 20 minutes or until toothpick inserted in center comes out clean. Immediately remove from pan. Serve warm.

Yield: 30 muffins
High Altitude (Above 3,500 Feet): No change.

Tip: *To substitute for buttermilk, use 2 tablespoons and 1½ teaspoons vinegar or lemon juice plus milk to make 2½ cups.

Nutrition Information Per Serving

Serving Size: 1 Muffin. Calories 150 • Calories from Fat 35 • Total Fat 4 g • Saturated Fat 1 g • Cholesterol 15 mg • Sodium 140 mg • Dietary Fiber 2 g Dietary Exchanges: 1 Starch, ½ Fruit, 1 Fat OR 1½ Carbohydrate, 1 Fat

Whole Wheat Pumpkin Muffins

Prep Time: 20 minutes
(Ready in 40 minutes)

Muffins

1½ cups whole wheat flour
½ cup firmly packed brown
  sugar
2 teaspoons baking powder
1 teaspoon pumpkin pie spice
½ teaspoon salt
1 egg
½ cup skim milk
½ cup canned pumpkin
¼ cup oil
½ teaspoon grated orange peel
½ cup dried currants

Glaze

¼ cup powdered sugar
1 to 1½ teaspoons orange juice

1. Heat oven to 375°F. Line 12 muffin cups with paper baking cups or spray with nonstick cooking spray. In large bowl, combine flour, brown sugar, baking powder, pumpkin pie spice and salt; mix well.
2. In small bowl, beat egg until foamy. Add milk, pumpkin, oil and orange peel; blend well. Add to flour mixture; stir just until dry ingredients are moistened. Stir in currants. Fill paper-lined muffin cups ¾ full.
3. Bake at 375°F. for 15 to 18 minutes or until toothpick inserted in center comes out clean. Immediately remove from pan.
4. In small bowl, blend powdered sugar and enough orange juice for desired drizzling consistency. Drizzle over warm muffins. Serve warm.

Yield: 12 muffins
High Altitude (Above 3,500 Feet): No change.

Nutrition Information Per Serving
Serving Size: 1 Muffin. Calories 170 • Calories from Fat 45 • Total Fat 5 g •
Saturated Fat 1 g • Cholesterol 20 mg • Sodium 190 mg • Dietary Fiber 3 g
Dietary Exchanges: 1 Starch, 1 Fruit, 1 Fat OR 2 Carbohydrate, 1 Fat

About Powdered Sugar

Powdered sugar, also known as confectioners' sugar or "10x" sugar, is made from granulated sugar that's ground to a very fine, powdery consistency and blended with cornstarch to prevent clumping. Its smooth texture makes it ideal for uncooked glazes and frostings that would be grainy if made with ordinary granulated sugar. The two types of sugar are not interchangeable: don't substitute one for the other unless a recipe gives specific instructions for doing so.

Kitchen Tip

If the powdered sugar looks lumpy, sift it through a fine-mesh strainer before adding the orange juice.

Savory Muffins

Savory muffins? Yes! Home-made bread can make even an ordinary weeknight supper seem a little more special. They share the same easy prep, quick baking and warm-from-the-oven goodness that make sweet muffins so appealing.

Muffins speckled with herbs or enriched with cheese or even bits of ham are perfect accom-paniments for your favorite main courses.

Savory Muffins

Previous page: Mexicali Corn Muffins, page 90

Raisin, Wheat and Rye Muffins

Prep Time: 15 minutes
(Ready in 35 minutes)

1 cup all-purpose flour
½ cup whole wheat flour
½ cup medium rye flour
¼ cup sugar
3 teaspoons baking powder
½ teaspoon salt

½ teaspoon cinnamon
¼ teaspoon nutmeg
½ cup raisins
1 cup milk
½ cup oil
1 egg, slightly beaten

1. Heat oven to 375°F. Grease bottoms only of 12 muffin cups or line with paper baking cups. In large bowl, combine all-purpose flour, whole wheat flour, rye flour, sugar, baking powder, salt, cinnamon, nutmeg and raisins; mix well.

2. Add milk, oil and egg; stir just until dry ingredients are moistened. Fill greased muffin cups ⅔ full.

3. Bake at 375°F. for 15 to 20 minutes or until muffins are very light brown and toothpick inserted in center comes out clean. Immediately remove from pan. Serve warm.

Yield: 12 muffins
High Altitude (Above 3,500 Feet): Decrease baking powder to 2 teaspoons.
Bake at 400°F. for 15 to 20 minutes.

Nutrition Information Per Serving

Serving Size: 1 Muffin. Calories 210 • Calories from Fat 90 • Total Fat 10 g •
Saturated Fat 2 g • Cholesterol 20 mg • Sodium 230 mg • Dietary Fiber 2 g
Dietary Exchanges: 1½ Starch, 2 Fat OR 1½ Carbohydrate, 2 Fat

editor's favorite

About All-Purpose Flour

As its name suggests, all-purpose flour is suitable for most types of general baking. Bread flour, on the other hand, has a higher gluten content to give bread dough its stretchy quality. Pastry flour or cake flour is softer and contains less gluten to yield more tender baked products. Bleached and unbleached all-purpose flour may be used interchangeably according to your personal preference. Most people can't tell the difference after baking, anyway.

Recipe Variation

For darker muffins, make the batter with ¼ cup molasses instead of sugar.

Rye 'n Wheat Muffins

Prep Time: 15 minutes
(Ready in 35 minutes)

Healthy Hint

For the lowest fat per muffin, choose nonfat plain yogurt rather than a low-fat or whole milk version.

Menu Suggestion

Serve these whole-grain muffins with a hearty vegetable soup or corn chowder.

Recipe Variation

Omit the orange peel and stir in 1 teaspoon caraway seed or dill weed instead.

1 cup medium rye flour
1 cup whole wheat flour
1 teaspoon baking soda
½ teaspoon salt
1 teaspoon grated orange peel

⅓ cup oil
2 tablespoons honey
1 (8-oz.) container plain yogurt
2 eggs

1. Heat oven to 350°F. Grease bottoms only of 12 muffin cups or line with paper baking cups. In large bowl, combine rye flour, whole wheat flour, baking soda, salt and orange peel; mix well.

2. In small bowl, combine oil, honey, yogurt and eggs; blend well. Add to flour mixture; stir just until dry ingredients are moistened. Fill greased muffin cups ⅔ full.

3. Bake at 350°F. for 15 to 20 minutes or until golden brown. Immediately remove from pan. Serve warm.

Yield: 12 muffins
High Altitude (Above 3,500 Feet): No change.

Nutrition Information Per Serving

Serving Size: 1 Muffin. Calories 160 • Calories from Fat 70 • Total Fat 8 g •
Saturated Fat 1 g • Cholesterol 35 mg • Sodium 220 mg • Dietary Fiber 2 g
Dietary Exchanges: 1 Starch, 1½ Fat OR 1 Carbohydrate, 1½ Fat

---

Onion Rye Muffins

Prep Time: 15 minutes
(Ready in 35 minutes)

¾ cup chopped onions
½ cup margarine or butter
1¼ cups all-purpose flour
¾ cup medium rye flour
2 tablespoons sugar
3 teaspoons baking powder

¾ teaspoon salt
½ teaspoon caraway seed,
  crushed
½ cup milk
2 eggs

1. Heat oven to 400°F. Line 12 muffin cups with paper baking cups or grease. In small skillet, cook onions in margarine until tender. Set aside.
2. In large bowl, combine all-purpose flour, rye flour, sugar, baking powder, salt and caraway seed; mix well. Add milk, eggs and cooked onions; stir just until dry ingredients are moistened. Fill paper-lined muffin cups ⅔ full.
3. Bake at 400°F. for 15 to 20 minutes or until toothpick inserted in center comes out clean. Immediately remove from pan. Serve warm.

Yield: 12 muffins
High Altitude (Above 3,500 Feet): No change.

Nutrition Information Per Serving

Serving Size: 1 Muffin. Calories 170 • Calories from Fat 80 • Total Fat 9 g •
Saturated Fat 2 g • Cholesterol 35 mg • Sodium 360 mg • Dietary Fiber 1 g
Dietary Exchanges: 1 Starch, ½ Fruit, 1½ Fat OR 1½ Carbohydrate, 1½ Fat

---

About Rye Flour

Rye flour is best used in combination with all-purpose flour for proper rising. It's more perishable than all-purpose flour and is best stored in the refrigerator.

Kitchen Tip

To crush caraway seeds, a traditional mortar and pestle work well. Otherwise, place the seeds on a cutting board and crush them with a heavy cast-iron frying pan or the side of a chef's knife or cleaver.

Menu Suggestion

Serve rye muffins with baked ham and a dollop of mustard for a variation on ham-on-rye sandwiches, or accompany the muffins with a hearty peasant-style soup.

Pumpernickel Muffins

About Pumpernickel

Pumpernickel is made with rye flour and gets its dark color from the addition of a dark ingredient such as molasses, brown sugar and even the unsweetened cocoa of this recipe. As with rye bread, caraway seed is a natural complement to pumpernickel breads.

Recipe Variation

Add ½ cup minced walnuts to the batter.

Prep Time: 15 minutes
(Ready in 35 minutes)

1 cup all-purpose flour
1 cup medium rye flour
⅓ cup firmly packed dark brown or regular brown sugar
2 tablespoons unsweetened cocoa
3 teaspoons baking powder
½ teaspoon salt
½ cup raisins, if desired
½ teaspoon caraway seed, if desired
1¼ cups buttermilk*
¼ cup oil
1 tablespoon molasses
1 egg, beaten

1. Heat oven to 400°F. Grease bottoms only of 12 muffin cups or line with paper baking cups. In medium bowl, combine all-purpose flour, rye flour, brown sugar, cocoa, baking powder, salt, raisins and caraway seed; mix well.
2. In small bowl, combine buttermilk, oil, molasses and egg; blend well. Add to flour mixture; stir just until dry ingredients are moistened. Fill greased muffin cups ¾ full.
3. Bake at 400°F. for 15 to 20 minutes or until toothpick inserted in center comes out clean. Cool 1 minute; remove from pan. Serve warm.

Yield: 12 muffins
High Altitude (Above 3,500 Feet): No change.

Tip: *To substitute for buttermilk, use 3¾ teaspoons vinegar or lemon juice plus milk to make 1¼ cups.

Nutrition Information Per Serving

Serving Size: 1 Muffin. Calories 190 • Calories from Fat 50 • Total Fat 6 g • Saturated Fat 1 g • Cholesterol 20 mg • Sodium 250 mg • Dietary Fiber 2 g
Dietary Exchanges: 1½ Starch, ½ Fruit, 1 Fat OR 2 Carbohydrate, 1 Fat

---

Pumpernickel Muffins

Bell Pepper Rye Muffins

Prep Time: 15 minutes
(Ready in 35 minutes)

Ingredient Substitution

A yellow bell pepper makes a sweet stand-in for the red. As an alternative to sautéing a fresh pepper, use ½ cup chopped roasted red bell pepper and melt the ½ cup margarine before adding it to the batter. Roasted peppers can be purchased in jars or from the deli case (drain well before use).

Recipe Variation

As an alternative to the basil seasoning, mix 1 tablespoon caraway seed into the batter.

¾ cup chopped red bell pepper
½ cup margarine or butter
1¼ cups all-purpose flour
¾ cup medium rye flour
2 tablespoons sugar

3 teaspoons baking powder
¾ teaspoon salt
½ teaspoon dried basil leaves
½ cup milk
2 eggs

1. Heat oven to 400°F. Grease bottoms only of 12 muffin cups or line with paper baking cups. In small skillet over medium heat, cook bell pepper in margarine until crisp-tender. Set aside.
2. In large bowl, combine all-purpose flour, rye flour, sugar, baking powder, salt and basil; mix well. In small bowl, combine milk, eggs and pepper mixture; mix well. Add to flour mixture; stir just until dry ingredients are moistened. Fill greased muffin cups ⅔ full.
3. Bake at 400°F. for 12 to 18 minutes or until toothpick inserted in center comes out clean. Immediately remove from pan. Serve warm.

Yield: 12 muffins
High Altitude (Above 3,500 Feet): No change.

Nutrition Information Per Serving
Serving Size: 1 Muffin. Calories 170 • Calories from Fat 80 • Total Fat 9 g • Saturated Fat 2 g • Cholesterol 35 mg • Sodium 360 mg • Dietary Fiber 1 g
Dietary Exchanges: 1 Starch, 2 Fat OR 1 Carbohydrate, 2 Fat

Basic Corn Muffins

Prep Time: 10 minutes
(Ready in 35 minutes)

1½ cups all-purpose flour
½ cup cornmeal
2 tablespoons sugar
3 teaspoons baking powder
¼ teaspoon salt

1 (7-oz.) can vacuum-packed
  whole kernel corn, well
  drained
1 cup milk
3 tablespoons oil
1 egg

1. Heat oven to 400°F. Line 12 muffin cups with paper baking cups. In medium bowl, combine flour, cornmeal, sugar, baking powder and salt; mix well. Stir in corn.
2. In small bowl, combine milk, oil and egg; blend well. Add to flour mixture; stir just until dry ingredients are moistened. Divide batter evenly into paper-lined muffin cups.
3. Bake at 400°F. for 18 to 23 minutes or until golden brown. Cool 1 minute; remove from pan. Serve warm.

Yield: 12 muffins
High Altitude (Above 3,500 Feet): No change.

Nutrition Information Per Serving
Serving Size: 1 Muffin. Calories 150 • Calories from Fat 45 • Total Fat 5 g •
Saturated Fat 1 g • Cholesterol 20 mg • Sodium 210 mg • Dietary Fiber 1 g
Dietary Exchanges: 1½ Starch, 1 Fat OR 1½ Carbohydrate, 1 Fat

---

Ingredient Substitution

In summer, 1 cup of cooked fresh corn on the cob may be used in place of the canned corn.

Recipe Variation

Stir 2 tablespoons chopped canned chile peppers into the batter. (Choose mild, medium or hot, according to your preference.)

Menu Suggestion

Serve these muffins with grilled steak and a salad of diced fresh tomatoes, minced basil and chives.

Cheesy Corn Muffins

Prep Time: 10 minutes
(Ready in 35 minutes)

1½ cups all-purpose flour
½ cup yellow cornmeal
¼ cup sugar
3 teaspoons baking powder
¼ teaspoon salt
1 cup milk
¼ cup oil

1 egg, slightly beaten
1 cup frozen whole kernel corn
or 7-oz. can vacuum-packed
whole kernel corn, drained
4 oz. (1 cup) shredded Cheddar
cheese

1. Heat oven to 400°F. Grease bottoms only of 12 muffin cups. In medium bowl, combine flour, cornmeal, sugar, baking powder and salt; blend well.

2. Add milk, oil and egg; stir just until dry ingredients are moistened. Fold in corn and cheese. Divide batter evenly into greased muffin cups.

3. Bake at 400°F. for 20 to 25 minutes or until golden brown. Immediately remove from pan. Serve warm.

Yield: 12 muffins
High Altitude (Above 3,500 Feet): No change.

Nutrition Information Per Serving

Serving Size: 1 Muffin. Calories 210 • Calories from Fat 80 • Total Fat 9 g •
Saturated Fat 3 g • Cholesterol 30 mg • Sodium 240 mg • Dietary Fiber 1 g
Dietary Exchanges: 1½ Starch, 2 Fat OR 1½ Carbohydrate, 2 Fat

---

Kitchen Tip

To keep a basket of muffins warm at the table, heat an unglazed clay tile in the oven while the muffins bake. Place the tile in the bottom of the basket, cover it with a hot pad or folded kitchen towel, then line the basket with another kitchen towel and add the muffins.

Menu Suggestion

These muffins will dress up a lunch of vegetable soup and a tossed salad.

Cheesy Corn Muffins

Blueberry Corn Muffins

Prep Time: 10 minutes
(Ready in 35 minutes)

About White Cornmeal

Although yellow cornmeal is most commonly seen, white and even blue cornmeal are also available. White cornmeal has a sweeter, milder flavor than yellow, but the two may be used interchangeably.

Recipe Variation

Make the muffins with 1 cup peeled, minced fresh peaches or nectarines instead of blueberries.

1¼ cups all-purpose flour
¾ cup white cornmeal
½ cup sugar
3 teaspoons baking powder
½ teaspoon salt
¾ cup milk

¼ cup margarine or butter, melted
1 egg, slightly beaten
1 cup fresh or frozen blueberries (do not thaw)

1. Heat oven to 400°F. Grease 12 muffin cups. In large bowl, combine flour, cornmeal, sugar, baking powder and salt; mix well.
2. Add milk, margarine and egg; stir just until dry ingredients are moistened. (Batter will be thin.) Gently stir in blueberries. Fill greased muffin cups ⅔ full.
3. Bake at 400°F. for 20 to 25 minutes or until light golden brown. Cool 1 minute; remove from pan. Serve warm.

Yield: 12 muffins
High Altitude (Above 3,500 Feet): Increase flour to 1⅓ cups. Bake as directed above.

Nutrition Information Per Serving
Serving Size: 1 Muffin. Calories 170 • Calories from Fat 45 • Total Fat 5 g •
Saturated Fat 1 g • Cholesterol 20 mg • Sodium 270 mg • Dietary Fiber 1 g
Dietary Exchanges: 1 Starch, 1 Fruit, 1 Fat OR 2 Carbohydrate, 1 Fat

Coriander Corn Muffins

Prep Time: 30 minutes

1½ cups all-purpose flour
½ cup yellow cornmeal
¼ cup sugar
¼ cup firmly packed brown sugar
3 teaspoons baking powder
½ teaspoon coriander

¼ teaspoon salt
½ cup skim milk
¼ cup oil
2 egg whites
1 cup frozen whole kernel corn, thawed*

1. Heat oven to 400°F. Spray 12 muffin cups with non-stick cooking spray, or line muffin cups with paper baking cups and spray paper cups with nonstick cooking spray.
2. In large bowl, combine flour, cornmeal, sugar, brown sugar, baking powder, coriander and salt; mix well.
3. In small bowl, combine milk, oil and egg whites; blend well. Add to flour mixture all at once; stir just until dry ingredients are moistened. Gently stir in corn. Divide batter evenly into sprayed muffin cups.
4. Bake at 400°F. for 14 to 19 minutes or until muffins are light golden brown and toothpick inserted in center comes out clean. Immediately remove from pan. Serve warm.

Yield: 12 muffins
High Altitude (Above 3,500 Feet): Decrease baking powder to 2 teaspoons.
Bake as directed above.

Tip: *To quickly thaw corn, place in colander or strainer; rinse with warm water until thawed. Drain well.

Nutrition Information Per Serving
Serving Size: 1 Muffin. Calories 170 • Calories from Fat 45 • Total Fat 5 g •
Saturated Fat 1 g • Cholesterol 0 mg • Sodium 180 mg • Dietary Fiber 1 g
Dietary Exchanges: 1 Starch, 1 Fruit, ½ Fat OR 2 Carbohydrate, ½ Fat

About Coriander

Coriander seed comes from the same plant that gives us fresh coriander leaves, which are also called cilantro or Chinese parsley. The seeds and leaves are not inter-changeable! The seeds have a warm, almost cit-rusy flavor, and are most notably used in baked sweets.

Kitchen Tip

Try a spring-release ice-cream scoop to fill the muffin cups neatly.

Ingredient Substitution

Change the character of the muffins by using 1 cup raisins or currants instead of corn kernels.

Mexicali Corn Muffins

(Pictured on page 76)

Prep Time: 10 minutes
(Ready in 35 minutes)

About Canned Chiles

Canned chiles are a useful nonperishable to keep on hand to add liveliness to recipes without bothering with fresh peppers. Unless you're a chile fanatic, little cans will be most useful, since most recipes call for only a small amount. Check the label and choose the heat level that appeals to you: mild, medium or hot. Drain the liquid before chopping. Store leftovers covered in the refrigerator.

Healthy Hint

To trim a few grams of fat, use nonfat plain yogurt in place of the sour cream and skim milk in place of the regular milk in this recipe.

Menu Suggestion

These zesty muffins are great with a hearty bowl of chili and cold Mexican beer or iced tea.

1¼ cups all-purpose flour
¾ cup cornmeal
2 tablespoons sugar
4 teaspoons baking powder
½ teaspoon salt
¾ cup milk

¼ cup sour cream
¼ cup oil
1 egg
1 (4-oz.) can chopped green
   chiles, drained

1. Heat oven to 400°F. Line 12 muffin cups with paper baking cups or grease. In large bowl, combine flour, cornmeal, sugar, baking powder and salt; mix well.

2. In medium bowl, combine milk, sour cream, oil, egg and chiles; beat well. Add to flour mixture; stir just until dry ingredients are moistened. Fill paper-lined muffin cups ⅔ full.

3. Bake at 400°F. for 18 to 22 minutes or until toothpick inserted in center comes out clean. Immediately remove from pan. Serve warm.

Yield: 12 muffins
High Altitude (Above 3,500 Feet): No change.

Nutrition Information Per Serving

Serving Size: 1 Muffin. Calories 160 • Calories from Fat 60 • Total Fat 7 g • Saturated Fat 2 g • Cholesterol 20 mg • Sodium 270 mg • Dietary Fiber 1 g
Dietary Exchanges: 1 Starch, ½ Fruit, 1 Fat OR 1½ Carbohydrate, 1 Fat

---

Jalapeño Jack Corn Muffins

Prep Time: 30 minutes

¾ cup skim milk
½ cup buttermilk*
2 tablespoons margarine or butter, melted
1 egg or ¼ cup refrigerated or frozen fat-free egg product, thawed
1½ cups all-purpose flour
½ cup yellow cornmeal

1 tablespoon sugar
2 teaspoons baking powder
½ teaspoon baking soda
½ teaspoon salt
3 oz. jalapeño Monterey Jack cheese, cut into 12 (¾-inch) cubes

1. Heat oven to 425°F. Spray 12 muffin cups with non-stick cooking spray or line with paper baking cups and spray paper cups. In medium bowl, combine skim milk, buttermilk, margarine and egg; blend well.

2. In large bowl, combine flour, cornmeal, sugar, baking powder, baking soda and salt; mix well. Push dry ingredients to sides of bowl to form well in center. Add milk mixture; stir just until dry ingredients are moistened. Divide batter evenly into sprayed muffin cups, filling each ⅔ to ¾ full. Press 1 cheese cube into center of each.

3. Bake at 425°F. for 10 to 15 minutes or until golden brown and firm to the touch. Immediately remove from pan; cool slightly. Serve warm.

Yield: 12 muffins
High Altitude (Above 3,500 Feet): No change.

Tip: *To substitute for buttermilk, use 1½ teaspoons vinegar or lemon juice plus skim milk to make ½ cup.

Nutrition Information Per Serving

Serving Size: 1 Muffin. Calories 140 • Calories from Fat 45 • Total Fat 5 g •
Saturated Fat 2 g • Cholesterol 25 mg • Sodium 310 mg • Dietary Fiber 1 g
Dietary Exchanges: 1 Starch, 1 Fat OR 1 Carbohydrate, 1 Fat

About Fat-Free Egg Product

Although they're usually called "egg substitutes," fat-free egg products are in fact made mostly of real egg whites. They contribute some of the egg's binding, leavening and texture-enhancing properties without the fat of a whole egg.

Ingredient Substitution

If hot peppers have too much kick for you, use regular Monterey Jack in place of the jalapeño-spiked version.

Menu Suggestion

For a summer cookout, these savory muffins go well with grilled steak, a tomato-lettuce salad and tall glasses of iced tea with wedges of lemon and sprigs of mint.

Chile Corn Sticks

About Blue Cornmeal

Blue cornmeal has a strong corn flavor and is made from a special variety of blue field corn. Look for it in specialty markets and health food stores.

Make It Special

As a change-of-pace spread, blend ricotta cheese with minced roasted red pepper and shredded fresh basil.

Menu Suggestion

Serve these corn sticks with grilled burgers or steak and a salad of fresh tomatoes, basil and chopped red onion. Wash it down with ice-cold lemonade or beer.

2 slices bacon, diced
¼ cup finely chopped onion
½ cup all-purpose flour
½ cup yellow or blue cornmeal
2 teaspoons sugar
2 teaspoons baking powder
½ teaspoon salt
½ cup milk
2 tablespoons oil
2 tablespoons chopped green chiles, drained
1 egg, beaten

1. Heat oven to 400°F. Grease corn stick pans or eight 2½-inch muffin cups. In small skillet, cook bacon and onion over medium heat until bacon is crisp and onion is tender. Drain; set aside.
2. In medium bowl, combine flour, cornmeal, sugar, baking powder and salt; mix well. Add bacon mixture and all remaining ingredients; stir just until dry ingredients are moistened. Divide batter evenly into greased stick pans.
3. Bake at 400°F. for 8 to 10 minutes or until toothpick inserted in center comes out clean. Cool 1 minute; remove from pans. Serve warm.

Yield: 12 corn sticks or 8 muffins
High Altitude (Above 3,500 Feet): No change.

Nutrition Information Per Serving
Serving Size: 1 Corn Stick. Calories 80 • Calories from Fat 35 • Total Fat 4 g • Saturated Fat 1 g • Cholesterol 20 mg • Sodium 200 mg • Dietary Fiber 1 g
Dietary Exchanges: ½ Starch, 1 Fat OR ½ Carbohydrate, 1 Fat

Jumbo Dilled Cornmeal Muffins

Prep Time: 15 minutes
(Ready in 35 minutes)

½ cup all-purpose flour
½ cup whole wheat flour
1 cup cornmeal
3 teaspoons baking powder
½ teaspoon salt
1 cup milk

¼ cup oil
3 tablespoons honey
2 tablespoons finely chopped
   fresh dill or 1 tablespoon
   dried dill weed
1 egg

1. Heat oven to 400°F. Grease six 6-oz. custard cups or 12 muffin cups; place custard cups in 15 × 10 × 1-inch baking pan. In large bowl, combine all-purpose flour, whole wheat flour, cornmeal, baking powder and salt; mix well.

2. In small bowl, combine milk, oil, honey, dill and egg; blend well. Add to flour mixture; stir just until dry ingredients are moistened. Divide batter evenly into greased custard cups.

3. Bake at 400°F. for 15 to 18 minutes or until toothpick inserted in center comes out clean. Cool 1 minute; remove from custard cups. Serve warm.

Yield: 6 jumbo muffins
High Altitude (Above 3,500 Feet): No change.

Nutrition Information Per Serving

Serving Size: 1 Jumbo Muffin. Calories 300 • Calories from Fat 110 • Total Fat 12 g • Saturated Fat 2 g • Cholesterol 40 mg • Sodium 460 mg • Dietary Fiber 3 g Dietary Exchanges: 2 Starch, 1 Fruit, 2 Fat OR 3 Carbohydrate, 2 Fat

---

• fiber source   • gift idea

About Dill Weed

Dill "weed" is the feathery top of the same plant that yields flavorful dill seeds. To use the fresh herb, pinch the delicate sprigs off the coarse stalks. Rinse, dry thoroughly by rolling the herbs in paper towels, then chop as directed.

Healthy Hint

Substitute skim milk for whole milk to trim the fat in these muffins.

Menu Suggestion

Serve the muffins with chicken stew and steamed green beans.

Strawberry Buttermilk Corn Muffins

Prep Time: 15 minutes
(Ready in 35 minutes)

½ cup dried strawberries
1 cup buttermilk*
2 tablespoons skim milk
2 tablespoons oil
1 egg or ¼ cup refrigerated or frozen fat-free egg product, thawed

1 cup all-purpose flour
1 cup yellow cornmeal
¼ cup sugar
2 teaspoons baking powder
½ teaspoon baking soda

Ingredient Substitution

Dried strawberries are available at specialty food stores and some health food shops. If you can't find them, substitute another dried fruit, such as cranberries, raisins or blueberries.

Menu Suggestion

Serve these muffins with strawberry jam, whipped butter and fresh fruit as a pretty accompaniment to scrambled eggs.

1. Heat oven to 400°F. Spray 12 muffin cups with non-stick cooking spray or line with paper baking cups.
2. In small bowl, cut dried strawberries into bite-sized pieces; set aside. In medium bowl, combine buttermilk, skim milk, oil and egg; blend well. Set aside.
3. In large bowl, combine flour, cornmeal, sugar, baking powder and baking soda; mix well. Push dry ingredients to sides of bowl to form well in center. Add egg mixture; stir just until dry ingredients are moistened. Gently stir in dried strawberries. Divide batter evenly into sprayed muffin cups, filling each ⅔ to ¾ full.
4. Bake at 400°F. for 12 to 18 minutes or until muffins are golden brown and toothpick inserted in center comes out clean. Immediately remove from pan; cool slightly. Serve warm.

Yield: 12 muffins
High Altitude (Above 3,500 Feet): No change.

Tip: *To substitute for buttermilk, use 1 tablespoon vinegar or lemon juice plus milk to make 1 cup.

Nutrition Information Per Serving
Serving Size: 1 Muffin. Calories 150 • Calories from Fat 35 • Total Fat 4 g • Saturated Fat 1 g • Cholesterol 20 mg • Sodium 170 mg • Dietary Fiber 2 g
Dietary Exchanges: 1 Starch, ½ Fruit, 1 Fat OR 1½ Carbohydrate, 1 Fat

Cheddar and Canadian Bacon Muffins

Prep Time: 15 minutes
(Ready in 35 minutes)

1 cup all-purpose flour
2 teaspoons freeze-dried
    chopped chives
1 teaspoon baking powder
¼ teaspoon garlic powder
⅓ cup milk
¼ cup sour cream

2 tablespoons oil
1 egg
2 oz. (½ cup) shredded
    Cheddar cheese
¼ cup finely chopped Canadian
    bacon or ham

1. Heat oven to 400°F. Grease 6 muffin cups, or line with paper baking cups and spray with nonstick cooking spray. In large bowl, combine flour, chives, baking powder and garlic powder; mix well.

2. In small bowl, combine milk, sour cream, oil and egg; beat well. Add to flour mixture; stir just until dry ingredients are moistened. Fold in cheese and bacon. Divide batter evenly into greased muffin cups.

3. Bake at 400°F. for 17 to 20 minutes or until toothpick inserted in center comes out clean. Immediately remove from pan. Serve warm.

Yield: 6 muffins
High Altitude (Above 3,500 Feet): No change.

Nutrition Information Per Serving

Serving Size: 1 Muffin. Calories 200 • Calories from Fat 100 • Total Fat 11 g •
Saturated Fat 4 g • Cholesterol 55 mg • Sodium 250 mg • Dietary Fiber 1 g
Dietary Exchanges: 1 Starch, ½ Lean Meat, 2 Fat OR 1 Carbohydrate,
½ Lean Meat, 2 Fat

Ingredient Substitution

2 tablespoons snipped fresh chives may be used in place of the freeze-dried.

Healthy Hint

Use nonfat plain yogurt instead of sour cream to reduce the fat in this recipe, and choose lean ham instead of regular.

Menu Suggestion

Offer these hearty savory muffins at brunch with scrambled eggs and fresh fruit salad.

Plump Carrot Muffins

Kitchen Tip

For the nicest flavor, make this recipe with fresh orange juice. Grate the peel of the orange before squeezing the fruit.

Healthy Hint

These muffins contain far less fat than typical carrot muffins and a lot more beta-carotene (vitamin A). Bake and freeze a batch to warm in the microwave or toaster oven on busy days.

Make It Special

To serve these moist muffins for dessert, top each with a dab of ready-to-serve orange-flavored frosting.

Prep Time: 20 minutes
(Ready in 40 minutes)

1¾ cups all-purpose flour
⅓ cup firmly packed brown sugar
1 teaspoon baking powder
1 teaspoon baking soda
1 teaspoon cinnamon
¼ teaspoon salt
½ cup shredded carrot

¾ cup orange juice
2 tablespoons oil
1½ teaspoons grated orange peel
1 teaspoon vanilla
1 egg
⅓ cup golden raisins

1. Heat oven to 375°F. Spray bottoms only of 12 muffin cups with nonstick cooking spray or line with paper baking cups. In large bowl, combine flour, brown sugar, baking powder, baking soda, cinnamon and salt; mix well.
2. In small bowl, combine carrot, orange juice, oil, orange peel, vanilla and egg; blend well. Add to flour mixture; stir just until dry ingredients are moistened. Stir in raisins. Fill sprayed muffin cups ¾ full.
3. Bake at 375°F. for 15 to 18 minutes or until toothpick inserted in center comes out clean. Cool 1 minute; remove from pan. Serve warm.

Yield: 12 muffins
High Altitude (Above 3,500 Feet): Increase flour to 2 cups.
Divide batter evenly into 14 muffin cups. Bake as directed above.

Nutrition Information Per Serving

Serving Size: 1 Muffin. Calories 140 • Calories from Fat 25 • Total Fat 3 g • Saturated Fat 0 g • Cholesterol 20 mg • Sodium 200 mg • Dietary Fiber 1 g
Dietary Exchanges: 1 Starch, ½ Fruit, ½ Fat OR 1½ Carbohydrate, ½ Fat

Plump Carrot Muffins

Carrot-Zucchini Muffins

Prep Time: 10 minutes
(Ready in 35 minutes)

gift idea

2 cups all-purpose flour
1 cup rolled oats
¾ cup firmly packed brown
   sugar
3 teaspoons baking powder
½ teaspoon cinnamon
¼ teaspoon salt

⅔ cup skim milk
3 tablespoons oil
2 egg whites
1 cup finely shredded carrots
½ cup shredded unpeeled
   zucchini (1 small)

1. Heat oven to 400°F. Spray 12 muffin cups with non-stick cooking spray, or line muffin cups with paper baking cups and spray paper cups with nonstick cooking spray.

2. In large bowl, combine flour, oats, brown sugar, baking powder, cinnamon and salt; mix well.

3. In small bowl, combine milk, oil and egg whites; blend well. Add to dry ingredients all at once; stir just until dry ingredients are moistened. Stir in carrots and zucchini just until blended. Spoon batter evenly into sprayed muffin cups.

4. Bake at 400°F. for 16 to 21 minutes or until muffins are golden brown and toothpick inserted in center comes out clean. Immediately remove from pan. Serve warm.

Yield: 12 muffins
High Altitude (Above 3,500 Feet): Decrease brown sugar to ⅔ cup.
Bake at 400°F. for 18 to 22 minutes.

Nutrition Information Per Serving
Serving Size: 1 Muffin. Calories 200 • Calories from Fat 35 • Total Fat 4 g •
Saturated Fat 1 g • Cholesterol 0 mg • Sodium 150 mg • Dietary Fiber 2 g
Dietary Exchanges: 2 Starch, 1 Fat OR 2 Carbohydrate, 1 Fat

Make It Special

Mix up a bit of icing from powdered sugar and lemon juice or orange juice and pipe or spoon it onto the top of the muffins.

Recipe Variation

Add ½ cup raisins or dried currants and/or ½ cup minced walnuts or pecans to the batter for extra texture.

Healthy Hint

Leaving the skin on the zucchini adds fiber as well as color and texture to these muffins.

Cheese-Topped Pumpkin Muffins, page 44; Carrot-Zucchini Muffins; Cranberry Upside-Down Muffins, page 50

Parmesan Herb Muffins

Prep Time: 30 minutes

About Sage

Sage, with its greenish gray, velvety leaves, is extremely pungent. It's the dominant flavor in most "poultry seasoning" blends.

Kitchen Tip

To maximize the cheese flavor, grate fresh Parmesan just before needed. Use a fine-holed grater, food processor or even an ordinary blender.

Menu Suggestion

Serve the muffins with veal chops or roasted chicken and a side dish of steamed carrots and green beans.

2 cups all-purpose flour
¾ cup grated Parmesan cheese
1 tablespoon sugar
1½ teaspoons baking powder
½ teaspoon baking soda

½ teaspoon dried sage leaves, crumbled
½ cup chopped fresh parsley
1¼ cups buttermilk*
¼ cup margarine or butter, melted
1 egg, slightly beaten

1. Heat oven to 400°F. Grease bottoms only of 12 muffin cups or line with paper baking cups. In large bowl, combine flour, cheese, sugar, baking powder, baking soda, sage and parsley; mix well.

2. Add buttermilk, margarine and egg; stir just until dry ingredients are moistened. Fill greased muffin cups ⅔ full.

3. Bake at 400°F. for 15 to 20 minutes or until toothpick inserted in center comes out clean. Immediately remove from pan. Serve warm.

Yield: 12 muffins
High Altitude (Above 3,500 Feet): No change.

Tip: *To substitute for buttermilk, use 3¾ teaspoons vinegar or lemon juice plus milk to make 1¼ cups.

Nutrition Information Per Serving

Serving Size: 1 Muffin. Calories 160 • Calories from Fat 60 • Total Fat 7 g • Saturated Fat 2 g • Cholesterol 25 mg • Sodium 310 mg • Dietary Fiber 1 g Dietary Exchanges: 1½ Starch, 1 Fat OR 1½ Carbohydrate, 1 Fat

Lemony Herb Muffins

Prep Time: 30 minutes

1 cup all-purpose flour
1 cup whole wheat flour
¼ cup sugar
¼ cup chopped fresh chives
3 teaspoons baking powder
2 teaspoons grated lemon
   peel
¾ teaspoon dried basil or
   oregano leaves
½ teaspoon salt
1 cup milk
⅓ cup margarine or butter,
   melted
1 egg, slightly beaten

1. Heat oven to 400°F. Grease 12 muffin cups or line with paper baking cups. In large bowl, combine all-purpose flour, whole wheat flour, sugar, chives, baking powder, lemon peel, basil and salt; mix well.

2. Add milk, margarine and egg; stir just until dry ingredients are moistened. Fill greased muffin cups ⅔ full.

3. Bake at 400°F. for 13 to 18 minutes or until toothpick inserted in center comes out clean. Immediately remove from pan. Serve warm.

Yield: 12 muffins
High Altitude (Above 3,500 Feet): No change.

Nutrition Information Per Serving

Serving Size: 1 Muffin. Calories 150 • Calories from Fat 50 • Total Fat 6 g •
Saturated Fat 1 g • Cholesterol 20 mg • Sodium 290 mg • Dietary Fiber 2 g
Dietary Exchanges: 1 Starch, ½ Fruit, 1 Fat OR 1½ Carbohydrate, 1 Fat

---

About Chives

Chives, like their onion cousins, are a member of the lily family. They're rewarding for the busy gardener to grow because they thrive without care. Their oniony flavor becomes milder when cooked, and they add nice color to dishes.

Menu Suggestion

Serve these muffins, with their intriguing lemon and herb flavor, with grilled or broiled salmon and steamed asparagus.

Onion-Chive Muffins

About Onions

Choose onions that have firm, taut skins and no soft spots. At home, store onions in a cool, dark place where air can circulate—not in the refrigerator and not in a plastic bag, which can trap moisture that spoils onions. Do not store onions with potatoes, which have different humidity requirements and will hasten decay.

Kitchen Tip

To chop an onion efficiently, cut it in half through the stem end and pull off the brown peel. Place the onion on the work surface, cut side down, and make a series of cuts about ¼ inch apart, not quite cutting through to the stem. Then, give the onion ¼ turn and make another series of cuts, resulting in a "crosshatch" of cuts. Next, lay the onion on its side and slice it to make the crosshatch into little pieces.

¾ **cup chopped onions**
1½ **cups all-purpose flour**
¼ **cup chopped fresh chives**
2 **tablespoons sugar**
2 **teaspoons baking powder**
½ **teaspoon salt**
¼ **teaspoon baking soda**

1 **cup buttermilk***
¼ **cup oil**
¼ **cup refrigerated or frozen fat-free egg product, thawed, or 1 egg, slightly beaten**

1. Heat oven to 375°F. Grease bottoms only of 12 muffin cups or line with paper baking cups. Spray small skillet with nonstick cooking spray. Add onions; cook and stir over medium heat until crisp-tender. Set aside.

2. In large bowl, combine flour, chives, sugar, baking powder, salt and baking soda; mix well. In small bowl, combine cooked onions, buttermilk, oil and egg product; blend well. Add to flour mixture; stir just until dry ingredients are moistened. Fill greased muffin cups about ¾ full.

3. Bake at 375°F. for 12 to 14 minutes or until toothpick inserted in center comes out clean. (Muffins will be very light in color.) Immediately remove from pan. Serve warm.

Yield: 12 muffins
High Altitude (Above 3,500 Feet): No change.

Tip: *To substitute for buttermilk, use 1 tablespoon vinegar or lemon juice plus milk to make 1 cup.

Nutrition Information Per Serving

Serving Size: 1 Muffin. Calories 120 • Calories from Fat 45 • Total Fat 5 g • Saturated Fat 1 g • Cholesterol 0 mg • Sodium 230 mg • Dietary Fiber 1 g
Dietary Exchanges: 1 Starch, 1 Fat OR 1 Carbohydrate, 1 Fat

Onion-Chive Muffins

Bis

Popovers a

Old-fashioned baking powder biscuits, scones and popovers are delightfully versatile— homey enough to round out a family supper yet special enough to serve to company. All of these old-fashioned breads taste best warm from the oven.

cuits, Scones, nd Doughnuts

Biscuits, Scones, Popovers and Doughnuts

Previous page: Baking Powder Biscuits, page 108

Sugar-Crusted Sweet Potato Biscuits

Prep Time: 15 minutes
(Ready in 35 minutes)

2 cups all-purpose flour
3 teaspoons baking powder
½ teaspoon salt
4 tablespoons brown sugar
3 tablespoons shortening

⅔ cup skim milk
½ cup mashed canned or
   cooked sweet potato
⅓ cup light sour cream

1. Heat oven to 400°F. Spray cookie sheet with nonstick cooking spray.
2. In medium bowl, combine flour, baking powder, salt and 2 tablespoons of the brown sugar; mix well. With pastry blender or fork, cut in shortening until mixture is crumbly.
3. In small bowl, combine milk, sweet potato and sour cream; blend well. Add to flour mixture all at once; stir just until dry ingredients are moistened. (If dough is too dry, add additional milk 1 teaspoon at a time, until all dry ingredients are moistened.) To form each biscuit, drop ¼ cup dough onto sprayed cookie sheet. Sprinkle with remaining 2 tablespoons brown sugar.
4. Bake at 400°F. for 15 to 20 minutes or until peaks and bottoms of biscuits are golden brown. Serve warm.

Yield: 12 biscuits
High Altitude (Above 3,500 Feet): No change.

Nutrition Information Per Serving
Serving Size: 1 Biscuit. Calories 150 • Calories from Fat 35 • Total Fat 4 g •
Saturated Fat 1 g • Cholesterol 2 mg • Sodium 230 mg • Dietary Fiber 1 g
Dietary Exchanges: 1 Starch, ½ Fruit, 1 Fat OR 1½ Carbohydrate, 1 Fat

About Nonstick Cooking Spray

Nonstick cooking spray is real vegetable oil in a can with a propellant that makes it possible for a little oil to go a long way. Because the oil droplets can be dispersed so finely, you need very little to grease a pan. Refillable canisters now on the market make it possible to create your own nonstick cooking spray from any kind of cooking oil.

Menu Suggestion

The sweet biscuits are a natural for breakfast and snacktime, but also work well with a meal of glazed baked ham, steamed sugar snap peas and a garden salad.

Baking Powder Biscuits

Kitchen Tip

Add the milk gradually to form a biscuit dough that sticks together but can still be handled. If you add too much milk, drop the dough onto the cookie sheet by large spoonfuls instead of rolling it and cutting it. Dropped biscuits will have a rough, irregular top.

Kitchen Tip

Use a light touch! While gently kneading the biscuit dough helps distribute the leavening for even rising and baking, too much toughens it.

2 cups all-purpose flour
3 teaspoons baking powder
½ teaspoon salt

½ cup shortening
¾ to 1 cup milk

1. Heat oven to 450°F. In large bowl, combine flour, baking powder and salt; mix well. With pastry blender or fork, cut in shortening until mixture resembles coarse crumbs. Stirring with fork, add enough milk so mixture leaves sides of bowl and forms a soft, moist dough.
2. On floured surface, toss dough lightly until no longer sticky. Roll or press dough to ½-inch thickness. Cut with floured 2-inch round cutter. Place on ungreased cookie sheet.
3. Bake at 450°F. for 8 to 12 minutes or until light golden brown. Serve warm.

Yield: 14 biscuits
High Altitude (Above 3,500 Feet): No change.

Food Processor Directions:

1. In food processor bowl with metal blade, combine flour, baking powder and salt. Process with 5 on/off pulses to mix. Add shortening to flour mixture. Process until mixture resembles coarse crumbs. Add ½ to ⅔ cup milk; process with on/off pulses just until ball starts to form.
2. On lightly floured surface, roll or press dough to ½-inch thickness. Cut with floured 2-inch round cutter. Continue as directed above.

Nutrition Information Per Serving
Serving Size: 1 Biscuit. Calories 140 • Calories from Fat 70 • Total Fat 8 g •
Saturated Fat 2 g • Cholesterol 0 mg • Sodium 190 mg • Dietary Fiber 0 g
Dietary Exchanges: 1 Starch, 1½ Fat OR 1 Carbohydrate, 1½ Fat

---

Variations

Buttermilk Biscuits: Add ¼ teaspoon baking soda to flour. Substitute buttermilk for milk.

Cheese Biscuits: Add 4 oz. (1 cup) shredded Cheddar cheese to flour-shortening mixture. Bake on greased cookie sheet.

Drop Biscuits: Increase milk to 1¼ cups. Drop dough by spoonfuls onto greased cookie sheets.

Soft-Sided Biscuits: Place biscuits in 9-inch round or square pan or on cookie sheet with sides touching. Bake at 450°F. for 12 to 14 minutes.

Southern-Style Biscuits: Decrease shortening to ¼ cup.

Thin-Crispy Biscuits: Roll dough to ¼-inch thickness. Cut biscuits with floured 3-inch round cutter.

Storage Tip

Baking powder biscuits are best warm from the oven, but leftovers can be reheated in the toaster oven for a nice breakfast treat.

Gorgonzola Cheese Biscuits

Prep Time: 35 minutes

2 cups all-purpose flour
3 teaspoons baking powder
½ teaspoon sugar
¼ teaspoon salt
¼ teaspoon baking soda

¼ teaspoon nutmeg
⅓ cup margarine or butter
4 oz. crumbled gorgonzola cheese
¾ to 1 cup buttermilk*

1. Heat oven to 425°F. Grease cookie sheet. In large bowl, combine flour, baking powder, sugar, salt, baking soda and nutmeg; mix well. With pastry blender or fork, cut in margarine and cheese until mixture resembles coarse crumbs.

2. Add ¾ cup buttermilk; stir with fork until mixture leaves sides of bowl and forms a soft, moist dough, adding additional buttermilk if necessary.

3. On floured surface, toss dough lightly until no longer sticky. Roll or press dough to ½-inch thickness; cut with floured 2-inch round cutter. Place on greased cookie sheet with sides touching.

4. Bake at 425°F. for 10 to 15 minutes or until light golden brown. Serve warm.

Yield: 18 biscuits
High Altitude (Above 3,500 Feet): No change.

Tip: *To substitute for buttermilk, use 2¼ to 3 teaspoons vinegar or lemon juice plus milk to make ¾ to 1 cup.

Nutrition Information Per Serving

Serving Size: 1 Biscuit. Calories 110 • Calories from Fat 45 • Total Fat 5 g • Saturated Fat 2 g • Cholesterol 5 mg • Sodium 270 mg • Dietary Fiber 0 g
Dietary Exchanges: 1 Starch, ½ Fat OR 1 Carbohydrate, ½ Fat

Gorgonzola Cheese Biscuits

Parmesan Herb Biscuits

Prep Time: 30 minutes

2 cups all-purpose flour
1/4 cup chopped fresh parsley
3 tablespoons grated Parmesan
  cheese
1 tablespoon sugar
3 teaspoons baking powder

1/2 teaspoon salt
1/2 teaspoon dried sage leaves
3/4 to 1 cup half-and-half
1 tablespoon margarine or
  butter, melted

1. Heat oven to 425°F. In large bowl, combine flour, parsley, 2 tablespoons of the cheese, sugar, baking powder, salt and sage; mix well. Add 3/4 cup half-and-half; stir with fork just until dry ingredients are moistened, adding additional half-and-half 1 tablespoon at a time, if necessary to form a soft dough.

2. On floured surface, gently knead dough to form a smooth ball. Pat dough into 1/2-inch-thick square. Using knife, cut into 12 squares; place on ungreased cookie sheet. Brush with melted margarine; sprinkle with remaining 1 tablespoon cheese.

3. Bake at 425°F. for 8 to 14 minutes or until light golden brown. Serve warm.

Yield: 12 biscuits
High Altitude (Above 3,500 Feet): Decrease baking powder to 2 teaspoons.
Bake as directed above.

Nutrition Information Per Serving

Serving Size: 1 Biscuit. Calories 120 • Calories from Fat 35 • Total Fat 4 g •
Saturated Fat 2 g • Cholesterol 10 mg • Sodium 260 mg • Dietary Fiber 1 g
Dietary Exchanges: 1 Starch, 1 Fat OR 1 Carbohydrate, 1 Fat

Kitchen Tip

The cutting technique outlined for these muffins works well for almost any rolled biscuit dough recipe. By patting the dough into a square, then cutting it into biscuits with a knife, you eliminate the need for a biscuit cutter. Plus, there's no rerolling, which can toughen the dough.

Menu Suggestion

These biscuits are great with veal parmigiana or Swiss steak and a tossed salad of romaine lettuce, red onion and ripe olives.

Parmesan Herb Biscuits

Carrot and Herb Dinner Biscuits

<table>
<tr><td>

1¼ **cups all-purpose flour**
¾ **cup cornmeal**
¼ **cup sugar**
3 **teaspoons baking powder**
1 **teaspoon dried basil leaves**
1 **teaspoon dried parsley flakes**

</td><td>

½ **teaspoon salt**
¾ **cup margarine or butter**
½ **cup shredded carrot**
⅓ **cup milk**
1 **egg, slightly beaten**

</td></tr>
</table>

1. Heat oven to 400°F. In medium bowl, combine flour, cornmeal, sugar, baking powder, basil, parsley flakes and salt; mix well. With pastry blender or fork, cut in margarine until mixture resembles coarse crumbs. Stir in carrot.

2. Add milk and egg; stir just until dry ingredients are moistened. To form each biscuit, drop ¼ cup of dough onto ungreased cookie sheet.

3. Bake at 400°F. for 12 to 14 minutes or until light golden brown. Serve warm.

Yield: 12 biscuits
High Altitude (Above 3,500 Feet): No change.

Nutrition Information Per Serving

Serving Size: 1 Biscuit. Calories 200 • Calories from Fat 110 • Total Fat 12 g • Saturated Fat 2 g • Cholesterol 20 mg • Sodium 360 mg • Dietary Fiber 1 g
Dietary Exchanges: 1 Starch, ½ Fruit, 2 Fat OR 1½ Carbohydrate, 2 Fat

---

Kitchen Tip

Shred the carrots on the finest-holed side of the grater for the best results with these biscuits.

Ingredient Substitution

One tablespoon each of minced fresh basil and parsley can substitute for the dried herbs.

Menu Suggestion

These herb-flecked biscuits nicely complement a supper of roast beef, steamed broccoli and tomato slices.

Carrot and Herb Dinner Biscuits

Jalapeño Corn Biscuits

Prep Time: 25 minutes

1½ cups all-purpose flour
¾ cup cornmeal
3 teaspoons baking powder
¼ teaspoon salt
½ cup shortening

1 cup milk
4 oz. (1 cup) shredded Monterey Jack cheese with jalapeño chiles

1. Heat oven to 450°F. Grease 2 cookie sheets. In large bowl, combine flour, cornmeal, baking powder and salt; mix well. With pastry blender or fork, cut in shortening until mixture resembles coarse crumbs.
2. Add milk and cheese; stir just until dry ingredients are moistened and soft dough forms. On floured surface, gently knead dough to form a smooth ball. Roll out to 1-inch thickness; cut with floured 2½-inch round cutter. Place on greased cookie sheets.
3. Bake at 450°F. for 9 to 13 minutes or until light golden brown. Serve warm.

Yield: 12 biscuits
High Altitude (Above 3,500 Feet): No change.

Tip: *To make drop biscuits, decrease flour to 1¼ cups. Drop dough by generous tablespoonfuls onto greased cookie sheets. Bake as directed above.

Nutrition Information Per Serving

Serving Size: 1 Biscuit. Calories 200 • Calories from Fat 110 • Total Fat 12 g • Saturated Fat 4 g • Cholesterol 10 mg • Sodium 230 mg • Dietary Fiber 1 g
Dietary Exchanges: 1½ Starch, 2 Fat OR 1½ Carbohydrate, 2 Fat

---

Sour Cream Drop Biscuits

Prep Time: 25 minutes

2 cups all-purpose flour
1 tablespoon sugar
3 teaspoons baking powder
½ teaspoon salt

¼ cup shortening
⅔ cup milk
⅔ cup sour cream

1. Heat oven to 450°F. Grease cookie sheet. In medium bowl, combine flour, sugar, baking powder and salt; mix well. With pastry blender or fork, cut in shortening until mixture is crumbly.
2. In small bowl, combine milk and sour cream; blend well. Add all at once to flour mixture; stir just until dry ingredients are moistened. Drop dough by tablespoonfuls onto greased cookie sheet.
3. Bake at 450°F. for 10 to 12 minutes or until golden brown. Serve warm.

Yield: 12 biscuits
High Altitude (Above 3,500 Feet): No change.

Nutrition Information Per Serving

Serving Size: 1 Biscuit. Calories 150 • Calories from Fat 60 • Total Fat 7 g •
Saturated Fat 3 g • Cholesterol 5 mg • Sodium 230 mg • Dietary Fiber 1 g
Dietary Exchanges: 1 Starch, 1½ Fat OR 1 Carbohydrate, 1½ Fat

Healthy Hint

Substitute nonfat plain yogurt for the sour cream and skim milk for the whole milk.

Menu Suggestion

Made with just a small amount of sugar, these flaky, light-textured biscuits could be served with jam for a sweet addition to the breakfast table. They can also hold their own alongside a supper of broiled chicken breasts, steamed mixed vegetables and coleslaw.

Garden Vegetable Drop Biscuits

About Zucchini

With its dark green skin and pale green interior, zucchini imparts color, fiber, texture, vitamins and flavor to these cheesy biscuits. At the market, choose firm unblemished zucchini that are small to medium in size. Larger zucchini tend to be watery. Store them unwrapped in the refrigerator produce drawer.

Make It Special

At the table, serve another container of the same cheese spread used in the biscuit dough.

1¾ cups all-purpose flour
2 teaspoons baking powder
½ teaspoon garlic salt
⅛ teaspoon pepper
⅔ cup milk

1 (5-oz.) container garden vegetable or herb-flavored soft spreadable cheese
1 egg, beaten
¾ cup shredded unpeeled zucchini

1. Heat oven to 400°F. Grease cookie sheet. In large bowl, combine flour, baking powder, garlic salt and pepper; mix well.
2. In small bowl, combine milk, cheese and egg; blend well with wire whisk. Stir in zucchini. Add to flour mixture; stir just until dry ingredients are moistened. To form each biscuit, drop ¼ cup dough onto greased cookie sheet.
3. Bake at 400°F. for 15 to 20 minutes or until golden brown. Serve warm.

Yield: 10 biscuits
High Altitude (Above 3,500 Feet): Increase flour to 2 cups.
Bake as directed above. Yields 12 biscuits.

Nutrition Information Per Serving

Serving Size: 1 Biscuit. Calories 150 • Calories from Fat 50 • Total Fat 6 g • Saturated Fat 4 g • Cholesterol 35 mg • Sodium 300 mg • Dietary Fiber 1 g
Dietary Exchanges: 1½ Starch, 1 Fat OR 1½ Carbohydrate, 1 Fat

Currant-Cardamom Scones

gift idea

Prep Time: 15 minutes
(Ready in 40 minutes)

1½ cups all-purpose flour
¼ cup sugar
3 teaspoons baking powder
½ teaspoon cardamom
¼ teaspoon salt
¼ cup margarine or butter

⅓ cup dried currants
2 teaspoons grated orange peel
½ cup buttermilk*
1 egg
1 teaspoon sugar

1. Heat oven to 400°F. In medium bowl, combine flour, ¼ cup sugar, baking powder, cardamom and salt; mix well. With pastry blender or fork, cut in margarine until mixture is crumbly. Stir in currants and orange peel.

2. In small bowl, combine buttermilk and egg; blend well. Add all at once; stir just until dry ingredients are moistened.

3. On well-floured surface, gently knead dough 5 or 6 times. Place on ungreased cookie sheet; press into 8-inch round, about 1 inch thick. Cut into 8 wedges; do not separate. Sprinkle with 1 teaspoon sugar.

4. Bake at 400°F. for 15 to 25 minutes or until light golden brown. Cut into wedges. Serve warm.

Yield: 8 scones

High Altitude (Above 3,500 Feet): Increase flour to 1¾ cups. Bake as directed above.

Tip: *To substitute for buttermilk, use 1½ teaspoons vinegar or lemon juice plus milk to make ½ cup.

Nutrition Information Per Serving

Serving Size: 1 Scone. Calories 200 • Calories from Fat 60 • Total Fat 7 g •
Saturated Fat 1 g • Cholesterol 25 mg • Sodium 340 mg • Dietary Fiber 1 g
Dietary Exchanges: 1½ Starch, ½ Fruit, 1 Fat OR 2 Carbohydrate, 1 Fat

---

About Dried Currants

Dried currants resemble miniature raisins. Like raisins, they are also dried from grapes. Raisins and currants may be used interchangeably in recipes, though currants have a more delicate, elegant appearance.

About Cardamom

Cardamom seems to be underappreciated in the United States, though this aromatic spice is extremely popular in the cuisines of Scandinavia, Germany, India, Indonesia and the Middle East. It's available in two forms: ground or whole. Whole cardamom pods hold the flavorful seeds with papery husks. Rub or crush the pod with your fingers to reveal the clusters of pungent seeds within. Use a mortar and pestle to grind the seeds.

Make It Special

Why not serve an elegant breakfast some leisurely Sunday morning? Break out the good china and teacups and serve Sugar-Crusted Orange Scones with strong coffee. Fill champagne glasses with fresh berries or sliced fruit. Start the day with a celebration!

Menu Suggestion

Serve these sweet scones with Cranberry-Orange Butter (page 230), or orange marmalade.

Sugar-Crusted Orange Scones

Prep Time: 15 minutes
(Ready in 40 minutes)

Scones
1 cup all-purpose flour
¼ cup sugar
¼ cup quick-cooking rolled oats
1 teaspoon baking powder
2 teaspoons grated orange peel
⅛ teaspoon salt
3 tablespoons butter
1 egg
¼ cup orange juice

Topping
1 teaspoon butter, melted
2 teaspoons sugar

1. Heat oven to 375°F. Grease cookie sheet. In medium bowl, combine flour, ¼ cup sugar, oats, baking powder, orange peel and salt; mix well. With pastry blender or fork, cut in 3 tablespoons butter until mixture is crumbly.

2. In small bowl, beat egg slightly; beat in orange juice. Add to flour mixture all at once; stir just until dry ingredients are moistened.

3. With floured hands, form mixture into 6-inch round on greased cookie sheet. Score top into 4 wedges; do not cut through. Brush with 1 teaspoon melted butter; sprinkle with 2 teaspoons sugar.

4. Bake at 375°F. for 12 to 22 minutes or until edges are golden brown. Cut into wedges along score lines. Serve warm.

Yield: 4 scones
High Altitude (Above 3,500 Feet): No change.

Nutrition Information Per Serving
Serving Size: 1 Scone. Calories 300 • Calories from Fat 100 • Total Fat 11 g • Saturated Fat 6 g • Cholesterol 80 mg • Sodium 300 mg • Dietary Fiber 2 g
Dietary Exchanges: 2 Starch, 1 Fruit, 2 Fat OR 3 Carbohydrate, 2 Fat

Scottish Scones

Prep Time: 15 minutes
(Ready in 45 minutes)

Scones
1½ cups all-purpose flour
¾ cup rolled oats
¼ cup firmly packed brown
    sugar
2 teaspoons baking powder
½ teaspoon salt
½ teaspoon cinnamon

½ cup margarine or butter
½ cup milk

Topping
1 tablespoon margarine or
    butter, melted
1 tablespoon sugar
¼ teaspoon cinnamon

1. Heat oven to 375°F. Lightly grease cookie sheet. In medium bowl, combine flour, oats, brown sugar, baking powder, salt and ½ teaspoon cinnamon; mix well. With pastry blender or fork, cut in ½ cup margarine until mixture is crumbly. Add milk all at once; stir just until dry ingredients are moistened.

2. On floured surface, gently knead dough 5 or 6 times. Place on greased cookie sheet; press into 6-inch round, about 1 inch thick. Brush top with melted margarine.

3. In small bowl, combine sugar and ¼ teaspoon cinnamon; mix well. Sprinkle over top. Cut into 8 wedges; separate slightly.

4. Bake at 375°F. for 20 to 30 minutes or until golden brown. Serve warm.

Yield: 8 scones
High Altitude (Above 3,500 Feet): No change.

Nutrition Information Per Serving
Serving Size: 1 Scone. Calories 270 • Calories from Fat 130 • Total Fat 14 g • Saturated Fat 3 g • Cholesterol 0 mg • Sodium 420 mg • Dietary Fiber 2 g Dietary Exchanges: 1½ Starch, ½ Fruit, 2½ Fat OR 2 Carbohydrate, 2½ Fat

Orange-Glazed Tropical Fruit Scones

About Dried Fruit Medleys

Almost any combination of dried fruit goes well in these "tropical" scones. It's especially fun to use a mixture of authentic island fruit, including dried pineapple, banana, mango, starfruit and papaya. "Regular" mixes are fine, too, with their more expected combination of dried apples, raisins, prunes and apricots.

Make It Special

To gild the lily, serve the scones with a crown of real whipped cream, perhaps flavored with a dash of Grand Marnier or another orange liqueur.

Prep Time: 40 minutes

Scones
2 cups all-purpose flour
2 tablespoons sugar
3 teaspoons baking powder
1 teaspoon salt
1½ teaspoons grated orange peel
¼ cup butter or margarine
⅓ cup milk
2 eggs, beaten

1 cup tropical medley dried fruit or dried fruit bits
½ cup white vanilla chips

Glaze
1 cup powdered sugar
2 to 3 tablespoons orange juice

Spread
⅓ cup apricot-pineapple or apricot preserves

1. Heat oven to 400°F. In large bowl, combine flour, sugar, baking powder, salt and orange peel; mix well. With pastry blender or fork, cut in butter until mixture resembles coarse crumbs.
2. Add milk and eggs; blend well. Stir in dried fruit and vanilla chips until well mixed.
3. On lightly floured surface, knead dough 6 or 7 times until smooth. Divide dough in half; pat each half into 6-inch round. With floured knife, cut each round into 4 wedges. Place wedges 2 inches apart on ungreased cookie sheet.
4. Bake at 400°F. for 12 to 16 minutes or until golden brown. Remove from cookie sheet; cool 1 minute.
5. Meanwhile, in small bowl, blend powdered sugar and enough orange juice for desired drizzling consistency. Drizzle mixture over top and sides of each scone. Cool 5 minutes. If desired, split each scone and spread with 2 teaspoons preserves, or serve preserves with scones. Serve warm.

Yield: 8 scones
High Altitude (Above 3,500 Feet): Increase flour to 2 cups plus 2 tablespoons.
Bake at 400°F. for 14 to 19 minutes or until golden brown.

Nutrition Information Per Serving

Serving Size: 1 Scone. Calories 430 • Calories from Fat 130 • Total Fat 14 g •
Saturated Fat 8 g • Cholesterol 70 mg • Sodium 550 mg • Dietary Fiber 2 g
Dietary Exchanges: 2 Starch, 2½ Fruit, 2½ Fat OR 4½ Carbohydrate, 2½ Fat

Orange-Glazed Tropical Fruit Scones

Blueberry Oat Scones

Prep Time: 15 minutes
(Ready in 40 minutes)

editor's favorite ● gift idea ●

Scones
1½ cups all-purpose flour
¾ cup quick-cooking rolled
   oats
⅓ cup sugar
2 teaspoons baking powder
¼ teaspoon salt
¼ teaspoon nutmeg
⅓ cup margarine or butter
1 egg

½ cup orange juice
½ teaspoon grated orange peel
1 cup fresh or frozen
   blueberries (do not thaw)

Topping
1 tablespoon margarine or
   butter, melted
2 tablespoons sugar

Make It Special

For an after-dinner treat, top warm Blueberry Oat Scones with a scoop of vanilla ice cream and drizzle with blueberry syrup.

Recipe Variation

Substitute lemon juice and lemon peel for the orange.

1. Heat oven to 375°F. Grease cookie sheet. In medium bowl, combine flour, oats, ⅓ cup sugar, baking powder, salt and nutmeg; mix well. With pastry blender or fork, cut in ⅓ cup margarine until mixture resembles coarse crumbs.

2. In small bowl, beat egg slightly. Add orange juice and orange peel; beat well. Add to flour mixture; stir just until blended. Stir in blueberries.

3. On floured surface, gently knead dough to make a smooth ball. Place on greased cookie sheet. With floured hands, press dough into 8-inch round. Cut into 8 wedges; do not separate. Brush with 1 tablespoon melted margarine; sprinkle with 2 tablespoons sugar.

4. Bake at 375°F. for 20 to 25 minutes or until golden brown. Cut into wedges. Serve warm.

Yield: 8 scones
High Altitude (Above 3,500 Feet): No change.

Nutrition Information Per Serving
Serving Size: 1 Scone. Calories 270 • Calories from Fat 90 • Total Fat 10 g •
Saturated Fat 2 g • Cholesterol 25 mg • Sodium 300 mg • Dietary Fiber 2 g
Dietary Exchanges: 1½ Starch, 1 Fruit, 2 Fat OR 2½ Carbohydrate, 2 Fat

Blueberry Oat Scones

Cherry-Pistachio Scones

Prep Time: 35 minutes
(Ready in 1 hour 10 minutes)

Make It Special

For a Christmas brunch, accent the red and green of the cherries and pistachios by sprinkling red and green decorator's sugar on top before baking.

Kitchen Tip

As an alternative to cutting a circle of scone dough into wedges, pat the dough into a rectangle and cut the dough into diamond shapes.

About Pistachios

Pistachios' natural color ranges from creamy to true green, with darker green being an indication of higher quality. Pistachios that are red have had their shells dyed.

2 cups all-purpose flour
2 tablespoons sugar
3 teaspoons baking powder
¾ teaspoon cinnamon
½ cup butter
¾ cup chopped drained maraschino cherries
½ cup chopped shelled pistachios
½ cup milk
1 egg, separated
4 teaspoons coarse sugar

1. Heat oven to 375°F. Line cookie sheet with parchment paper or lightly grease cookie sheet. In large bowl, combine flour, sugar, baking powder and cinnamon; mix well. With pastry blender or fork, cut in butter until mixture resembles coarse crumbs. Stir in cherries and pistachios.
2. In small bowl, combine milk and egg yolk; blend well. Add to flour mixture; stir just until dry ingredients are moistened.
3. On lightly floured surface, gently knead dough several times. Divide dough in half; place on paper-lined cookie sheet. Pat each half into 6-inch round. Cut each round into 6 wedges; do not separate.
4. In small bowl, beat egg white. Brush over tops of scones. Sprinkle with coarse sugar.
5. Bake at 375°F. for 17 to 22 minutes or until golden brown. Remove from cookie sheet; cool 10 minutes. Cut into wedges. Serve warm.

Yield: 12 scones
High Altitude (Above 3,500 Feet): No change.

Nutrition Information Per Serving

Serving Size: 1 Scone. Calories 220 • Calories from Fat 100 • Total Fat 11 g • Saturated Fat 5 g • Cholesterol 40 mg • Sodium 210 mg • Dietary Fiber 1 g • Dietary Exchanges: 1½ Starch, 2 Fat OR 1½ Carbohydrate, 2 Fat

Cherry-Pistachio Scones

Cranberry-Walnut Scones

Prep Time: 20 minutes
(Ready in 50 minutes)

About Dried Cranberries

A relative newcomer to the dried fruit scene, dried cranberries are now available in most supermarkets. Most brands have been sweetened to compensate for the berries' natural tartness. They can be used in many recipes as a measure-for-measure substitute for raisins.

Make It Special

Sift a little powdered sugar over the top just before serving.

Recipe Variation

Use ¾ cup orange juice in place of buttermilk.

Ingredient Substitution

To substitute for buttermilk, use 2 teaspoons vinegar or lemon juice plus milk to make ¾ cup.

Cranberry-Walnut Scones

2 cups all-purpose flour
2 tablespoons sugar
2 teaspoons baking powder
1 teaspoon freshly grated nutmeg or nutmeg
½ teaspoon baking soda
½ teaspoon salt
½ cup unsalted butter, butter or margarine
1 (3.53-oz.) pkg. (½ cup) sweetened dried cranberries
½ cup chopped walnuts
¾ cup buttermilk
1 egg, separated
2 teaspoons sugar

1. Heat oven to 375°F. Lightly grease cookie sheet or line with parchment paper. In large bowl, combine flour, 2 tablespoons sugar, baking powder, nutmeg, baking soda and salt; mix well. With pastry blender or fork, cut in butter until mixture resembles coarse crumbs. Stir in cranberries and walnuts.

2. In small bowl, combine buttermilk and egg yolk; blend well. Add to flour mixture; stir just until dry ingredients are moistened.

3. On lightly floured surface, gently knead dough 12 times. Divide dough in half; place on greased cookie sheet. Pat each half into a 6-inch round. Cut each into 6 wedges; do not separate.

4. In small bowl, beat egg white slightly. Brush over tops of scones. Sprinkle with 2 teaspoons sugar.

5. Bake at 375°F. for 15 to 20 minutes or until golden brown. Remove from cookie sheet; cool 10 minutes. Cut into wedges. Serve warm.

Yield: 12 scones
High Altitude (Above 3,500 Feet): No change.

Nutrition Information Per Serving
Serving Size: 1 Scone. Calories 230 • Calories from Fat 110 • Total Fat 12 g • Saturated Fat 5 g • Cholesterol 40 mg • Sodium 250 mg • Dietary Fiber 1 g
Dietary Exchanges: 1½ Starch, 2½ Fat OR 1½ Carbohydrate, 2½ Fat

Twelfth Night Scones

Prep Time: 20 minutes
(Ready in 45 minutes)

Recipe Fact

Twelfth Night is celebrated on January 6, twelve days after Christmas. It commemorates the arrival of the three kings at the stable in Bethlehem.

Ingredient Substitution

To substitute for buttermilk, use 1 teaspoon vinegar or lemon juice plus milk to make ⅓ cup.

Storage Tip

Purchase butter on sale and store extra sticks in the freezer. Although it takes butter a long time to actually spoil in the refrigerator, it loses its fresh flavor within a week or so because it picks up odors from other stored foods.

Scones

1¾ cups all-purpose flour
¼ cup sugar
2 teaspoons baking powder
¼ teaspoon baking soda
¼ teaspoon salt
¼ cup butter
½ cup sweetened dried cranberries
½ cup white vanilla chips
1 teaspoon grated orange peel
½ cup low-fat vanilla yogurt
⅓ cup buttermilk

Topping

1 to 2 tablespoons buttermilk or milk
1 tablespoon sugar
½ teaspoon grated orange peel

1. Heat oven to 375°F. Grease cookie sheet. In large bowl, combine flour, ¼ cup sugar, baking powder, baking soda and salt; mix well. With pastry blender or fork, cut in butter until mixture resembles coarse crumbs. Stir in cranberries, vanilla chips and 1 teaspoon orange peel. Add yogurt and ⅓ cup buttermilk; stir just until dry ingredients are moistened.
2. Shape dough into ball; place on greased cookie sheet. Roll or pat dough into 8-inch round. Cut into 8 wedges; do not separate.
3. Brush dough with 1 to 2 tablespoons buttermilk. In small bowl, combine 1 tablespoon sugar and ½ teaspoon orange peel; mix well. Sprinkle over dough.
4. Bake at 375°F. for 15 to 20 minutes or until edges are light golden brown. Remove from cookie sheet; cool 5 minutes. Cut into wedges. Serve warm.

Yield: 8 scones
High Altitude (Above 3,500 Feet): Increase flour to 2 cups. Bake as directed above.

Nutrition Information Per Serving

Serving Size: 1 Scone. Calories 290 • Calories from Fat 90 • Total Fat 10 g •
Saturated Fat 6 g • Cholesterol 20 mg • Sodium 320 mg • Dietary Fiber 1 g
Dietary Exchanges: 2 Starch, 1 Fruit, 1½ Fat OR 3 Carbohydrate, 1½ Fat

Middleberry Scones

Scones

1½ cups all-purpose flour
½ cup whole wheat flour
2 tablespoons sugar
3 teaspoons baking powder
½ teaspoon salt
½ teaspoon cinnamon
1 teaspoon grated orange peel
¼ cup butter or margarine
⅔ cup half-and-half

1 egg
⅓ cup raspberry preserves
1 teaspoon sugar

Spread and Garnish

1 (3-oz.) pkg. cream cheese, softened
16 fresh raspberries or strawberries
1 teaspoon grated orange peel

Kitchen Tip

Leave the cream cheese at room temperature for an hour to soften, or give it a brief zap (remove the foil wrapper first) in the microwave.

Healthy Hint

Half-and-half in the dough yields tender, rich-tasting scones, but most people won't be able to tell the difference if you substitute skim milk, plus you'll trim a few grams of fat along the way.

1. Heat oven to 425°F. Lightly grease cookie sheet. In large bowl, combine all-purpose flour, whole wheat flour, 2 tablespoons sugar, baking powder, salt, cinnamon and 1 teaspoon orange peel; mix well. With pastry blender or fork, cut in butter until mixture resembles coarse crumbs.
2. In small bowl, combine half-and-half and egg; blend well. Add to flour mixture; stir just until dry ingredients are moistened.
3. On well-floured surface, gently knead dough 4 times. Divide dough in half; pat each half into 8-inch round. Place 1 round on greased cookie sheet; spread preserves to within 1 inch of edge. Place remaining round over preserves; pinch edges to seal. Sprinkle top with 1 teaspoon sugar. Cut into 8 wedges; do not separate.
4. Bake at 425°F. for 15 to 18 minutes or until edges are golden brown. Cut into wedges. Serve warm with cream cheese. Garnish with fresh berries and 1 teaspoon orange peel.

Yield: 8 scones
High Altitude (Above 3,500 Feet): No change.

Nutrition Information Per Serving

Serving Size: 1 Scone. Calories 290 • Calories from Fat 120 • Total Fat 13 g • Saturated Fat 8 g • Cholesterol 60 mg • Sodium 430 mg • Dietary Fiber 2 g • Dietary Exchanges: 2½ Starch, 2 Fat OR 2½ Carbohydrate, 2 Fat

Fruity Scones

Prep Time: 30 minutes

3¼ cups all-purpose flour
4 tablespoons sugar
2 teaspoons baking soda
1 teaspoon cream of tartar
1 teaspoon salt
1 tablespoon grated orange
   peel

6 tablespoons margarine or
   butter
1 (6-oz.) pkg. (1¼ cups) dried
   fruit bits
1 to 1¼ cups milk

1. Heat oven to 425°F. Lightly grease cookie sheets. In large bowl, combine flour, 3 tablespoons of the sugar, baking soda, cream of tartar, salt and orange peel; mix well. With pastry blender or fork, cut in margarine until mixture resembles coarse crumbs. Stir in dried fruit bits. Add milk; stir just until dry ingredients are moistened.
2. On lightly floured surface, gently knead dough 10 times. Roll or pat dough to ¾-inch thickness. Cut out scones with floured 3-inch round cutter; place 2 inches apart on greased cookie sheets. Sprinkle remaining 1 tablespoon sugar evenly over scones.
3. Bake at 425°F. for 7 to 12 minutes or until light golden brown. Serve warm.

Yield: 14 scones
High Altitude (Above 3,500 Feet): No change.

Nutrition Information Per Serving

Serving Size: 1 Scone. Calories 210 • Calories from Fat 50 • Total Fat 6 g •
Saturated Fat 1 g • Cholesterol 0 mg • Sodium 400 mg • Dietary Fiber 2 g
Dietary Exchanges: 1 Starch, 1½ Fruit, 1 Fat OR 2½ Carbohydrate, 1 Fat

About Cream of Tartar

Cream of tartar plus baking soda, the principal ingredients in commercial baking powders, undergo a chemical reaction when they come in contact with moisture: They produce carbon dioxide gas, which leavens dough. In recipes that call for beaten egg whites, a bit of cream of tartar added midway during beating will help stabilize the peaks so they don't deflate.

Kitchen Tip

A sharp-edged cookie cutter or biscuit cutter works best for shaping the dough. A drinking glass or other cutter with rounded edges will compress the sides of the scones and inhibit proper rising.

Fruity Scones

Savory Cheese and Scallion Scones

Prep Time: 20 minutes
(Ready in 55 minutes)

Scones

2³/₄ cups all-purpose flour
5 teaspoons baking powder
½ teaspoon salt, if desired
4 oz. (1 cup) crumbled feta cheese
4 oz. cream cheese, cut into 1-inch cubes

4 scallions or green onions, chopped
1 cup half-and-half or milk
1 egg

Glaze, if desired

1 egg
2 tablespoons milk

1. Heat oven to 400°F. Grease large cookie sheet. In large bowl, combine flour, baking powder and salt; mix well. With pastry blender or fork, cut in feta cheese and cream cheese until mixture is crumbly. Add scallions; toss gently until combined.

2. In small bowl, combine half-and-half and 1 egg; blend well. Add to flour mixture; stir gently, just until soft dough forms.

3. On well-floured surface, gently knead dough 5 or 6 times. Pat or press dough into 1-inch-thick round. With floured knife, cut into 8 wedges. Place wedges 2 inches apart on greased cookie sheet.

4. In small bowl, combine glaze ingredients; blend well. Brush over tops of scones.

5. Bake at 400°F. for 25 to 30 minutes or until golden brown. Remove from cookie sheet; cool 5 minutes. Serve warm or cool. Store in refrigerator.

Yield: 8 scones
High Altitude (Above 3,500 Feet): No change.

Nutrition Information Per Serving
Serving Size: 1 Scone. Calories 310 • Calories from Fat 120 • Total Fat 13 g •
Saturated Fat 8 g • Cholesterol 95 mg • Sodium 670 mg • Dietary Fiber 1 g
Dietary Exchanges: 2½ Starch, 2½ Fat OR 2½ Carbohydrate, 2½ Fat

About Scallions

Scallions are immature onions whose bulbs haven't yet had a chance to mature. Once the root end has been trimmed away, both the white end and the green leaves can be used. In many recipes, you can ignore instructions that dictate "white part only" or "green part only."

About Feta Cheese

Feta cheese is a Greek specialty made with sheep or goat's milk. Soft, crumbly and salty, it's used in Greek salads. Store it in the refrigerator, covered with water, changing the water every couple of days.

Make It Special

Sprinkle the top of each egg-glazed biscuit with sesame seed prior to baking.

Menu Suggestion

Serve the scones with your favorite main course soup for lunch or supper.

Fresh Herb Scones

Prep Time: 20 minutes
(Ready in 40 minutes)

2 cups all-purpose flour
¼ cup chopped fresh parsley
1 tablespoon sugar
1 tablespoon chopped fresh
    thyme or 1 teaspoon dried
    thyme leaves
3 teaspoons baking powder

1 teaspoon chopped fresh
    rosemary or ¼ teaspoon
    dried rosemary leaves,
    crushed
½ teaspoon salt
⅓ cup margarine or butter
½ cup milk
1 egg, slightly beaten

1. Heat oven to 400°F. Lightly grease cookie sheet. In large bowl, combine flour, parsley, sugar, thyme, baking powder, rosemary and salt; mix well. With pastry blender or fork, cut in margarine until mixture resembles coarse crumbs. Stir in milk and egg just until moistened.
2. On floured surface, gently knead dough 10 times. Place on greased cookie sheet; roll or pat dough into 6-inch round. Cut into 8 wedges; separate slightly.
3. Bake at 400°F. for 15 to 20 minutes or until golden brown. Serve warm.

Yield: 8 scones
High Altitude (Above 3,500 Feet): Decrease baking powder to 2 teaspoons.
Bake as directed above.

Nutrition Information Per Serving

Serving Size: 1 Scone. Calories 210 • Calories from Fat 80 • Total Fat 9 g •
Saturated Fat 2 g • Cholesterol 30 mg • Sodium 420 mg • Dietary Fiber 1 g
Dietary Exchanges: 1½ Starch, ½ Fruit, 1½ Fat OR 2 Carbohydrate, 1½ Fat

About Thyme

Thyme is a branchy herb with tiny, highly aromatic leaves that complement poultry and dried bean dishes. The leaves must be stripped from the fibrous stalks before use.

About Rosemary

Among the most assertive of herbs, rosemary comes from an evergreen plant whose leaves resemble pine needles. Strip them from the woody stems before use. Rosemary is best used with a judicious hand, since some people find it overpowering. In Italy, it's a traditional seasoning for roasted pork with garlic.

Menu Suggestion

These three-herb scones make a fine side dish for a meal of beef-vegetable soup or roasted pork.

Cornmeal Sage Scones

Prep Time: 15 minutes
(Ready in 45 minutes)

Kitchen Tip

Crumbling dried sage leaves just before using them maximizes the herb's flavor.

Make It Special

Blend 1 teaspoon of minced chives into 4 tablespoons softened butter to make a savory spread for the baked scones.

Menu Suggestion

These savory scones are perfect for a traditional Thanksgiving menu or a modified "Sunday dinner" version of roasted chicken and gravy, cranberry sauce, mashed potatoes and Brussels sprouts or another green vegetable.

1¼ cups all-purpose flour
½ cup yellow cornmeal
¼ cup grated Parmesan cheese
2 teaspoons baking powder
½ teaspoon baking soda
½ teaspoon salt
¾ teaspoon dried sage leaves, crumbled
¼ cup margarine or butter
¾ cup buttermilk*

1. Heat oven to 425°F. Spray cookie sheet with nonstick cooking spray. In large bowl, combine flour, cornmeal, cheese, baking powder, baking soda, salt and sage; mix well. With pastry blender or fork, cut in margarine until mixture resembles coarse crumbs. Add buttermilk; stir just until dry ingredients are moistened.
2. On lightly floured surface, gently knead dough 10 times. Place on sprayed cookie sheet; roll or pat dough into 6½-inch round. Cut into 8 wedges; do not separate.
3. Bake at 425°F. for 20 to 25 minutes or until light golden brown. Remove from cookie sheet; cool 5 minutes. Cut into wedges. Serve warm.

Yield: 8 scones
High Altitude (Above 3,500 Feet): No change.

Tip: *To substitute for buttermilk, use 2¼ teaspoons vinegar or lemon juice plus milk to make ¾ cup.

Nutrition Information Per Serving
Serving Size: 1 Scone. Calories 170 • Calories from Fat 60 • Total Fat 7 g • Saturated Fat 2 g • Cholesterol 3 mg • Sodium 490 mg • Dietary Fiber 1 g
Dietary Exchanges: 1½ Starch, 1 Fat OR 1½ Carbohydrate, 1 Fat

Cornmeal Sage Scones

Perfect Popovers

Prep Time: 10 minutes
(Ready in 1 hour)

3 eggs, room temperature
1¼ cups milk, room
   temperature

1¼ cups all-purpose flour
¼ teaspoon salt

1. Heat oven to 450°F. Generously grease 10 popover cups or 6-oz. custard cups.* In small bowl, beat eggs with eggbeater or wire whisk until lemon-colored and foamy. Add milk; blend well.
2. Add flour and salt; beat with eggbeater just until batter is smooth and foamy on top. Pour batter into greased cups, filling about ⅔ full.
3. Bake at 450°F. for 15 minutes. (DO NOT OPEN OVEN.) Reduce oven temperature to 350°F.; bake an additional 25 to 35 minutes or until high, hollow and deep golden brown. Remove from oven; insert sharp knife into each popover to allow steam to escape. Remove from cups. Serve warm.

Yield: 10 popovers

High Altitude (Above 3,500 Feet): Increase flour to 1¼ cups plus 2 tablespoons.
Bake at 450°F. for 15 minutes. Reduce oven temperature to 350°F.;
bake an additional 20 to 30 minutes.

Tip: *Greased standard muffin pans can be substituted for the popover cups. Fill every other greased cup with batter to prevent sides of popovers from touching.

Nutrition Information Per Serving
Serving Size: 1 Popover. Calories 90 • Calories from Fat 20 • Total Fat 2 g •
Saturated Fat 1 g • Cholesterol 65 mg • Sodium 90 mg • Dietary Fiber 0 g
Dietary Exchanges: 1 Starch, ½ Fat OR 1 Carbohydrate, ½ Fat

Recipe Fact

The classic popover is made with just four basic ingredients—eggs, milk, flour and salt—no leavener, no butter. The trademark hollow interior of the finished bread results from steam building up during baking and causing the batter to magically pop. For best results, use room-temperature eggs and milk and resist the temptation to open the oven door before the end of cooking time, especially at the critical juncture when the oven temperature is lowered to 350°F.

Make It Special

For an improvised rendition of profiteroles, which are usually made from choux pastry (cream-puff pastry) filled with ice cream, stuff the warm-from-the-oven popovers with vanilla ice cream and drizzle with chocolate syrup or fresh berries.

Perfect Popovers

Dill-Parmesan Popovers

low-fat

Ingredient Substitution

Flavor the batter with ½ teaspoon ground dried sage instead of dill to complement a meal of chicken or turkey.

Menu Suggestion

These savory popovers make a nice accompaniment for beef stew or meatloaf.

Prep Time: 10 minutes
(Ready in 1 hour)

3 eggs, room temperature
1¼ cups milk, room temperature
1¼ cups all-purpose flour

2 tablespoons grated Parmesan cheese
1 teaspoon dried dill weed
½ teaspoon salt

1. Heat oven to 450°F. Generously grease 8 popover cups or eight 6-oz. custard cups. In small bowl, beat eggs with eggbeater or wire whisk until lemon-colored and foamy. Add milk; blend well.

2. Add all remaining ingredients; beat with eggbeater just until batter is smooth and foamy on top. Pour batter into greased cups, filling each about ⅔ full.

3. Bake at 450°F. for 20 minutes. (DO NOT OPEN OVEN.) Reduce oven temperature to 350°F.; bake an additional 15 to 30 minutes or until deep golden brown. Remove from oven; insert sharp knife into each popover to allow steam to escape. Remove from cups. Serve warm.

Yield: 8 popovers
High Altitude (Above 3,500 Feet): No change.

Nutrition Information Per Serving

Serving Size: 1 Popover. Calories 120 • Calories from Fat 25 • Total Fat 3 g •
Saturated Fat 1 g • Cholesterol 85 mg • Sodium 200 mg • Dietary Fiber 1 g
Dietary Exchanges: 1 Starch, ½ Medium-Fat Meat OR
1 Carbohydrate, ½ Medium-Fat Meat

Mini Cheese 'n Chive Popovers

low-fat

Prep Time: 10 minutes
(Ready in 40 minutes)

2 eggs, room temperature
⅔ cup milk, room temperature
⅔ cup all-purpose flour
3 tablespoons finely shredded
    Cheddar cheese

1 tablespoon chopped fresh
    chives or 1 teaspoon freeze-
    dried chopped chives
⅛ teaspoon garlic powder
⅛ teaspoon salt

1. Heat oven to 450°F. Generously spray 18 miniature muffin cups with nonstick cooking spray. In small bowl, beat eggs with wire whisk or eggbeater until lemon-colored and foamy. Add milk; blend well.

2. Add all remaining ingredients; beat with wire whisk just until batter is smooth and foamy on top. Pour batter into sprayed cups, filling to within ¼ inch of top.

3. Bake at 450°F. for 10 minutes. (DO NOT OPEN OVEN.) Reduce oven temperature to 350°F.; bake an additional 10 to 20 minutes or until popovers are high and deep golden brown. Remove from oven; insert sharp knife into each popover to allow steam to escape. Remove from pan. Serve warm.

Yield: 18 mini popovers
High Altitude (Above 3,500 Feet): No change.

Nutrition Information Per Serving

Serving Size: 2 Mini Popovers. Calories 70 • Calories from Fat 20 • Total Fat 2 g •
Saturated Fat 1 g • Cholesterol 50 mg • Sodium 70 mg • Dietary Fiber 0 g
Dietary Exchanges: ½ Starch, ½ Fat OR ½ Carbohydrate, ½ Fat

Make It Special

Serve the popovers arranged on a pretty plate garnished with fresh pink chive flowers. The flowers, by the way, are also edible and share the green stems' oniony flavor. Extra flowers are a tasty addition to a tossed green salad.

Menu Suggestion

Make Roasted Garlic Spread (page 235) to accompany these savory popovers.

Cake Doughnuts

Prep Time: 40 minutes

Recipe Fact

If you're used to dough-nuts that taste like little more than sugar-coated white bread, you're in for a real treat. Homemade doughnuts bring back memories of the farm, even if you grew up in the city!

Kitchen Tip

If you don't have an electric frying pan, check the oil's temperature with a candy thermometer. If the oil is too cool, the dough-nut will be soggy and leaden; if the oil is too hot, the outside of the doughnut can burn before the inside is cooked. When the oil is just the right temperature, it "sears" the outside of the doughnut so that grease doesn't penetrate. The exterior will become deep golden brown while the inside cooks up tender and perfectly crumbed.

4 cups all-purpose flour	1 cup buttermilk*
1 cup sugar	¼ cup margarine or butter,
3 teaspoons baking powder	melted, or ¼ cup oil
1 teaspoon baking soda	1 teaspoon vanilla
1 teaspoon salt	2 eggs, slightly beaten
½ teaspoon nutmeg	Oil for deep frying

1. In large bowl, combine flour, sugar, baking powder, baking soda, salt and nutmeg; mix well. Add all remaining ingredients except oil for frying; stir just until dry ingredients are moistened. If desired, refrigerate dough for easier handling.

2. Fill large saucepan or electric skillet ⅔ full with oil. Heat to 375°F.

3. Meanwhile, on well-floured surface, knead dough 1 to 2 minutes or until no longer sticky. Roll half of dough at a time to ½-inch thickness. Cut with floured doughnut cutter.

4. With pancake turner, slip doughnuts and holes into hot oil (375°F.). Fry doughnuts and holes 1 to 1½ minutes on each side or until deep golden brown. Drain on paper towels. If desired, roll doughnuts and holes in powdered sugar, granulated sugar or a cinnamon-sugar mixture, or drizzle with glaze.

Yield: 30 doughnuts
High Altitude (Above 3,500 Feet): No change.

Tip: *To substitute for buttermilk, use 1 tablespoon vinegar or lemon juice plus milk to make 1 cup.

Nutrition Information Per Serving
Serving Size: 1 Doughnut. Calories 130 • Calories from Fat 45 • Total Fat 5 g • Saturated Fat 1 g • Cholesterol 15 mg • Sodium 190 mg • Dietary Fiber 0 g Dietary Exchanges: ½ Starch, 1 Fruit, 1 Fat OR 1½ Carbohydrate, 1 Fat

---

Chocolate Doughnuts

Prep Time: 40 minutes
(Ready in 1 hour 10 minutes)

Doughnuts
4 cups all-purpose flour
1¼ cups sugar
3 teaspoons baking powder
1 teaspoon baking soda
1 teaspoon salt
1 cup buttermilk
¼ cup oil
1 teaspoon vanilla
2 eggs, slightly beaten
1 oz. unsweetened chocolate,
melted
Oil for deep frying

Glaze
2 cups powdered sugar
2 tablespoons margarine or
butter, softened
2 oz. unsweetened chocolate,
melted, cooled
1 teaspoon vanilla
3 to 4 tablespoons milk

Kitchen Tips

To substitute for buttermilk, use 1 tablespoon vinegar or lemon juice plus milk to make 1 cup.

If desired, batter can be dropped by spoonfuls into hot fat. Omit chilling and rolling steps.

1. In large bowl, combine flour, sugar, baking powder, baking soda and salt; mix well. Add buttermilk, oil, 1 teaspoon vanilla, eggs and 1 ounce melted chocolate; stir just until dry ingredients are moistened. Cover dough; refrigerate 30 minutes for easier handling.
2. In deep fat fryer or large heavy saucepan, heat 2 to 3 inches of oil to 375°F.
3. Meanwhile, on well-floured surface, toss dough lightly until no longer sticky. Roll half of dough at a time to ½-inch thickness. Cut with floured doughnut cutter.
4. With pancake turner, slip doughnuts and holes into hot oil (375°F.). Fry 1 to 1½ minutes on each side or until deep golden brown. Drain on paper towels.
5. In a small bowl, blend remaining ingredients, adding enough milk for desired glaze consistency; blend until smooth. Dip each doughnut in glaze.

Yield: 30 doughnuts
High Altitude (Above 3,500 Feet): No change.

Nutrition Information Per Serving
Serving Size: 1 Doughnut. Calories 200 • Calories from Fat 70 • Total Fat 8 g •
Saturated Fat 2 g • Cholesterol 15 mg • Sodium 190 mg • Dietary Fiber 1 g
Dietary Exchanges: 1 Starch, 1 Fruit, 1½ Fat OR 2 Carbohydrate, 1½ Fat

Quick Breads

Part bread and part cake, quick breads are easy to make and satisfying to eat. Unlike the majority of muffins, which are best fresh from the oven, loaves generally have a longer shelf life. In fact, many of them benefit from sitting several hours or overnight for easier slicing. They also rank among the best gifts from the kitchen, since they're usually sturdy enough to be good travelers.

Quick Breads

*Previous page: Apricot-Date Bread, page 156;
Marmalade Butter, page 227*

Banana Bread

Prep Time: 15 minutes
(Ready in 2 hours 20 minutes)

¾ cup sugar
½ cup margarine or butter,
    softened
2 eggs
1 cup (2 medium) mashed ripe
    bananas

⅓ cup milk
1 teaspoon vanilla
2 cups all-purpose flour
½ cup chopped nuts, if desired
1 teaspoon baking soda
½ teaspoon salt

1. Heat oven to 350°F. Grease bottom only of 9 × 5 or 8 × 4-inch loaf pan. In large bowl, combine sugar and margarine; beat until light and fluffy. Add eggs; beat well. Add bananas, milk and vanilla; blend well.

2. In small bowl, combine flour, nuts, baking soda and salt; mix well. Add to banana mixture; stir just until dry ingredients are moistened. Pour into greased pan.

3. Bake at 350°F. for 50 to 60 minutes or until toothpick inserted in center comes out clean. Cool 5 minutes; remove from pan. Cool 1 hour or until completely cooled. Wrap tightly and store in refrigerator.

Yield: 1 (16-slice) loaf
High Altitude (Above 3,500 Feet): Increase flour to 2 cups plus 1 tablespoon.
Bake at 375°F. for 45 to 55 minutes.

Nutrition Information Per Serving
Serving Size: 1 Slice. Calories 190 • Calories from Fat 80 • Total Fat 9 g •
Saturated Fat 2 g • Cholesterol 25 mg • Sodium 220 mg • Dietary Fiber 1 g
Dietary Exchanges: 1 Starch, ½ Fruit, 1½ Fat OR 1½ Carbohydrate, 1½ Fat

Variation

Applesauce Bread: Substitute 1 cup applesauce for mashed bananas and add ¾ teaspoon cinnamon with flour.

About Bananas

In Central America and elsewhere in the tropics, bananas grow upside down in huge bunches that get divided into the individual "hands" we buy in supermarkets. Here's an interesting, though not very useful, fact: All bananas are perfectly tri-sectable lengthwise, meaning that they are segmented into three sections that run the length of the banana. Green bananas will ripen nicely on the counter at room temperature (do not refrigerate them).

Recipe Variation

Add ½ cup raisins or dried currants to the batter.

Menu Suggestion

Serve the loaf with Whipped Cream Cheese (page 231) and your favorite fruit preserves.

Nut Bread

Make It Special

For a nutty-but-nice theme gift, gather together a loaf of nut bread, a package of hazelnut-flavored coffee and a small jar of almond butter or another specialty nut butter. Throw in a package of roasted nuts for good measure.

Menu Suggestion

Set out slices of nut bread, whipped cream cheese and apricot preserves to round out a tea tray for a breakfast buffet or afternoon tea. Serve a plate of sliced navel oranges or fresh cherries alongside.

¾ cup sugar
½ cup margarine or butter, softened
1 cup buttermilk*
2 eggs

2 cups all-purpose flour
1 cup chopped nuts
½ teaspoon baking powder
½ teaspoon baking soda
½ teaspoon salt

1. Heat oven to 350°F. Grease bottom only of 9 × 5 or 8 × 4-inch loaf pan. In large bowl, combine sugar and margarine; beat until light and fluffy. Add buttermilk and eggs; blend well.

2. In small bowl, combine flour, nuts, baking powder, baking soda and salt; mix well. Add to buttermilk mixture; stir just until dry ingredients are moistened. Pour into greased pan.

3. Bake at 350°F. for 55 to 65 minutes or until toothpick inserted in center comes out clean. Cool 15 minutes; remove from pan. Cool 1 hour or until completely cooled. Wrap tightly and store in refrigerator.

Yield: 1 (16-slice) loaf
High Altitude (Above 3,500 Feet): Increase flour to 2 cups plus 1 tablespoon.
Bake at 375°F. for 50 to 60 minutes.

Tip: *To substitute for buttermilk, use 1 tablespoon vinegar or lemon juice plus milk to make 1 cup.

Nutrition Information Per Serving

Serving Size: 1 Slice. Calories 210 • Calories from Fat 100 • Total Fat 11 g • Saturated Fat 2 g • Cholesterol 25 mg • Sodium 210 mg • Dietary Fiber 1 g
Dietary Exchanges: 1½ Starch, 2 Fat OR 1½ Carbohydrate, 2 Fat

---

Variations

Date Bread: Substitute brown sugar for sugar; decrease nuts to ½ cup. Stir in 1 cup chopped dates and 1 teaspoon grated orange peel after flour addition.

Pocket of Streusel Bread: For filling, in small bowl, combine ½ cup firmly packed brown sugar, ½ cup chopped walnuts, 1 teaspoon cinnamon and 1 tablespoon margarine or butter, melted; mix well. Prepare batter as directed above, substituting brown sugar for sugar and decreasing nuts to ½ cup. Spread half of batter in greased and floured 9 × 5-inch loaf pan. Spoon filling down center of batter and spread to within ½ inch of all sides. Carefully spoon remaining batter over filling, spreading gently to cover. Bake at 350°F. for 50 to 55 minutes.

Eggnog Quick Bread

Prep Time: 15 minutes
(Ready in 2 hours 15 minutes)

About Eggnog

Traditional fresh eggnog is made from egg, cream and/or milk, sugar, sweet spices and, frequently, a splash of rum. Eggnog has become somewhat controversial in recent years because the egg and cream make it a high-calorie, high-cholesterol drink, and because the raw egg holds up the possibility of salmonella contamination. Purchased eggnog, on the other hand, is pasteurized, making it a safer drink. Read the Nutrition Facts panel on the carton to compare calories and fat with other beverages, and look for low-fat versions of this drink. Purchased eggnog is usually thick and rich enough that it's still delicious "cut" with plain or even skim milk.

Recipe Variation

Rum and raisins are a time-honored combination; stir ½ cup of raisins into the batter, if you wish.

2 eggs
1 cup sugar
1 cup dairy eggnog (not canned)
½ cup margarine or butter, melted

2 teaspoons rum extract
1 teaspoon vanilla
2¼ cups all-purpose flour
2 teaspoons baking powder
½ teaspoon salt
¼ teaspoon nutmeg

1. Heat oven to 350°F. Grease bottom only of 9 × 5-inch loaf pan.* Beat eggs in large bowl. Add sugar, eggnog, margarine, rum extract and vanilla; blend well.
2. Add flour, baking powder, salt and nutmeg; stir just until dry ingredients are moistened. Pour into greased pan.
3. Bake at 350°F. for 45 to 50 minutes or until toothpick inserted in center comes out clean. Cool 10 minutes; remove from pan. Cool 1 hour or until completely cooled. Wrap tightly and store in refrigerator.

Yield: 1 (16-slice) loaf
High Altitude (Above 3,500 Feet): No change.

Tip: *If desired, recipe can be baked in two 5¾ × 3¼-inch disposable foil or metal loaf pans. Grease bottoms only of pans. Bake at 350°F. for 35 to 40 minutes.

Nutrition Information Per Serving

Serving Size: 1 Slice. Calories 200 • Calories from Fat 70 • Total Fat 8 g • Saturated Fat 2 g • Cholesterol 35 mg • Sodium 210 mg • Dietary Fiber 0 g
Dietary Exchanges: 1 Starch, 1 Fruit, 1½ Fat OR 2 Carbohydrate, 1½ Fat

---

Eggnog Quick Bread

Sweet Cinnamon Quick Bread

Cinnamon comes from the inner bark of a tropical evergreen tree. Purchase it ground for all-purpose use in baked dishes or buy it in curled "sticks," which are good for flavoring pilafs, stews and mulled drinks; remove them before serving.

Kitchen Tip

To swirl the streusel mixture into the batter, sprinkle the mixture over the top of the dough, then use a butter knife to swirl the streusel into the batter without incorporating it completely.

Recipe Variation

Add ½ cup minced nuts and/or ½ cup miniature chocolate chips to the streusel mixture; sprinkle additional chocolate chips on top before baking.

Prep Time: 15 minutes
(Ready in 2 hours 25 minutes)

Bread
2 cups all-purpose flour
1 cup sugar
4 teaspoons baking powder
1½ teaspoons cinnamon
½ teaspoon salt
1 cup buttermilk*
⅓ cup oil

2 teaspoons vanilla
2 eggs

Streusel
2 tablespoons sugar
1 teaspoon cinnamon
2 teaspoons margarine or
   butter, softened

1. Heat oven to 350°F. Grease and flour bottom only of 9 × 5 or 8 × 4-inch loaf pan.

2. In large bowl, combine all bread ingredients; beat 3 minutes at medium speed. Pour batter into greased and floured pan. In small bowl, combine all streusel ingredients until crumbly. Sprinkle over batter; swirl to marble batter and streusel.

3. Bake at 350°F. for 45 to 55 minutes or until toothpick inserted in center comes out clean. Cool 15 minutes; remove from pan. Cool 1 hour or until completely cooled. Wrap tightly and store in refrigerator.

Yield: 1 (12-slice) loaf
High Altitude (Above 3,500 Feet): Bake at 375°F. for 45 to 50 minutes.

Tip: *To substitute for buttermilk, use 1 tablespoon vinegar or lemon juice plus milk to make 1 cup.

Nutrition Information Per Serving
Serving Size: 1 Slice. Calories 240 • Calories from Fat 70 • Total Fat 8 g • Saturated Fat 1 g • Cholesterol 35 mg • Sodium 290 mg • Dietary Fiber 1 g
Dietary Exchanges: 2 Starch, ½ Fruit, 1 Fat OR 2½ Carbohydrate, 1 Fat

Buttermilk Chocolate Bread

Prep Time: 15 minutes
(Ready in 2 hours 35 minutes)

1 cup sugar
½ cup margarine or butter, softened
2 eggs
1 cup buttermilk*
1¾ cups all-purpose flour

½ cup unsweetened cocoa
½ teaspoon baking powder
½ teaspoon baking soda
½ teaspoon salt
⅓ cup chopped nuts

1. Heat oven to 350°F. Grease bottom only of 8 × 4 or 9 × 5-inch loaf pan. In large bowl, combine sugar and margarine; blend well. Add eggs; beat well. Stir in buttermilk.

2. Add flour, cocoa, baking powder, baking soda and salt; stir just until dry ingredients are moistened. Stir in nuts. Pour into greased pan.

3. Bake at 350°F. for 55 to 65 minutes or until toothpick inserted in center comes out clean. Cool 15 minutes; remove from pan. Cool 1 hour or until completely cooled. Wrap tightly and store in refrigerator.

Yield: 1 (12-slice) loaf

High Altitude (Above 3,500 Feet): Increase flour to 1¾ cups plus 1 tablespoon. Bake at 375°F. for 50 to 55 minutes.

Tip: *To substitute for buttermilk, use 1 tablespoon vinegar or lemon juice plus milk to make 1 cup.

Nutrition Information Per Serving

Serving Size: 1 Slice. Calories 220 • Calories from Fat 100 • Total Fat 11 g • Saturated Fat 2 g • Cholesterol 35 mg • Sodium 280 mg • Dietary Fiber 2 g
Dietary Exchanges: 1½ Starch, 2 Fat OR 1½ Carbohydrate, 2 Fat

Make It Special

Diehard chocoholics can sprinkle chocolate chips on top of the loaf before baking. The sweet, melted chips add another dimension of chocolate.

About Cocoa Powder

Unsweetened cocoa powder is made from dried, ground chocolate liquor. Because it contains no cocoa butter, it contains no fat. Chocolate is actually slightly acidic, so recipes made with cocoa powder usually call for baking soda to neutralize the acid. Dutch-process cocoa has been "alkalized," which neutralizes the acidity and results in what many bakers consider a smoother texture.

Gingerbread Loaves

Prep Time: 20 minutes
(Ready in 3 hours 10 minutes)

Bread
¾ cup firmly packed brown
    sugar
½ cup butter, softened
2 eggs
1 cup molasses
½ cup boiling water
½ teaspoon baking soda
2¾ cups all-purpose flour
2 teaspoons baking powder

4 teaspoons ginger
2 teaspoons cinnamon
1 teaspoon allspice
1 teaspoon cloves
¼ teaspoon salt

Glaze
½ cup powdered sugar
1 to 2 tablespoons lemon juice

About Molasses

Molasses, a by-product of sugar refining, gives dark color and intense flavor to baked goods, and is the traditional sweetener for gingerbread. Try a little molasses on bread or toast as a switch from honey or jam.

Kitchen Tip

Powdered sugar has a tendency to become lumpy over time. Press it through a sieve, if necessary, for a smooth glaze.

1. Heat oven to 350°F. Grease two 8 × 4-inch loaf pans. In large bowl, combine brown sugar and butter; beat until light and fluffy. Add eggs; beat well.

2. In small bowl, combine molasses, water and baking soda; mix well. Beat into brown sugar mixture. Gradually add all remaining bread ingredients; mix well. Spoon batter into greased pans.

3. Bake at 350°F. for 40 to 50 minutes or until loaves spring back when touched lightly in the center. Cool 15 minutes; remove from pans. Cool 1¼ hours or until completely cooled.

4. In small bowl, combine glaze ingredients; blend well. Brush cooled loaves with glaze. Let stand 30 minutes or until glaze is set. Wrap tightly and store in refrigerator.

Yield: 2 (16-slice) loaves
High Altitude (Above 3,500 Feet): Decrease molasses to ¾ cup.
Increase water to 1 cup and flour to 3 cups. Bake as directed above.

Nutrition Information Per Serving
Serving Size: 1 Slice. Calories 130 • Calories from Fat 25 • Total Fat 3 g •
Saturated Fat 2 g • Cholesterol 20 mg • Sodium 105 mg • Dietary Fiber 0 g
Dietary Exchanges: 1 Starch, ½ Fruit, ½ Fat OR 1½ Carbohydrate, ½ Fat

Gingerbread Loaves

Apricot-Date Bread

Prep Time: 15 minutes
(Ready in 2 hours 35 minutes)

Make It Special

Drizzle the top of the warm loaf with a glaze made from powdered sugar and apricot brandy.

About Dates

Now widely grown in California, dates are native to the Sahara. They are nearly always sold dried, either whole or chopped, with or without pits.

Ingredient Substitution

Dried pears or apples are delicious stand-ins for the apricots.

½ cup dried apricots, cut into small thin strips
Boiling water
½ cup chopped dates
½ cup chopped walnuts
1 cup firmly packed brown sugar

1½ cups milk
¼ cup oil
1 egg
2¾ cups all-purpose flour
¾ teaspoon baking powder
¾ teaspoon baking soda
¾ teaspoon salt

1. Heat oven to 350°F. Grease and flour bottom only of 9 × 5-inch loaf pan. In small bowl, cover apricots with boiling water. Let stand 5 minutes. Drain; stir in dates and walnuts.

2. In large bowl, combine brown sugar, milk, oil and egg; blend well. Add flour, baking powder, baking soda and salt; stir just until dry ingredients are moistened. Stir in apricot mixture. Pour into greased and floured pan.

3. Bake at 350°F. for 60 to 70 minutes or until toothpick inserted in center comes out clean. Cool 10 minutes; remove from pan. Cool 1 hour or until completely cooled. Wrap tightly and store in refrigerator.

Yield: 1 (16-slice) loaf
High Altitude (Above 3,500 Feet): No change.

Nutrition Information Per Serving

Serving Size: 1 Slice. Calories 230 • Calories from Fat 60 • Total Fat 7 g • Saturated Fat 1 g • Cholesterol 15 mg • Sodium 200 mg • Dietary Fiber 2 g Dietary Exchanges: 1½ Starch, 1 Fruit, 1 Fat OR 2½ Carbohydrate, 1 Fat

Spicy Apple Bread

1 cup shreds of whole bran
   cereal
1 cup milk
¾ cup sugar
½ cup margarine or butter,
   softened
2 eggs
1½ cups all-purpose flour

3 teaspoons baking powder
½ teaspoon salt
½ teaspoon cinnamon
¼ teaspoon allspice
¼ teaspoon nutmeg
1 cup finely chopped, peeled
   apples

1. Heat oven to 375°F. Grease bottom only of 8 × 4 or 9 × 5-inch loaf pan. In small bowl, combine cereal and milk; mix well. Let stand 5 minutes.

2. In large bowl, combine sugar and margarine; beat until light and fluffy. Add eggs and cereal mixture; beat well. Add flour, baking powder, salt, cinnamon, allspice and nutmeg; mix well. Fold in apples. Pour batter into greased pan.

3. Bake at 375°F. for 50 to 60 minutes or until toothpick inserted in center comes out clean. Cool 10 minutes; remove from pan. Cool 1 hour or until completely cooled. Wrap tightly and store in refrigerator.

Yield: 1 (16-slice) loaf
High Altitude (Above 3,500 Feet): No change.

Nutrition Information Per Serving

Serving Size: 1 Slice. Calories 180 • Calories from Fat 60 • Total Fat 7 g • Saturated Fat 2 g • Cholesterol 30 mg • Sodium 250 mg • Dietary Fiber 2 g Dietary Exchanges: 1½ Starch, 1½ Fat OR 1½ Carbohydrate, 1½ Fat

About Allspice

Allspice is really a single spice; it gets its name from its flavor, which tastes like a combination of several sweet spices. It's most often used in combination with other sweet spices (cinnamon, nutmeg, cloves) to underscore and round out flavors. Because it's fairly assertive, allspice is typically used in smaller amounts than cinnamon.

Make It Special

The moist texture of this loaf makes it a good keeper and ideal gift. For a gift idea, line a basket with a new kitchen towel and tuck in a loaf of Spicy Apple Bread plus a couple of fresh apples. Mix and match deep red Delicious, green Granny Smith and Golden Delicious for a beautiful presentation.

Storage Tip

Wrap the cooled loaf tightly in plastic and refrigerate it overnight. The loaf is actually best served the second day, when the texture has firmed up a bit and the flavors have blended.

Cranberry Surprise Loaf

Prep Time: 20 minutes
(Ready in 2 hours 50 minutes)

Kitchen Tip

Softening cream cheese is the key to success in many recipes. If you have time to plan ahead, soften cream cheese by having it stand at room temperature for about an hour. When you're in a hurry, remove the cream cheese from its foil wrapper and soften it in the microwave, but do not allow it to melt.

Kitchen Tip

This loaf will slice best if it's completely cooled, preferably overnight in the refrigerator. For an attractive presentation, fan slices on a serving tray to show off the cream cheese layer in the center.

Recipe Variation

Make the loaf with ¾ cup orange juice and 1 teaspoon grated orange peel instead of the apple juice.

2 (3-oz.) pkg. cream cheese, softened
1 egg
2 cups all-purpose flour
1 cup sugar
1½ teaspoons baking powder
½ teaspoon baking soda
½ teaspoon salt
¾ cup apple juice
¼ cup margarine or butter, melted
1 egg, beaten
1½ cups coarsely chopped fresh cranberries*
½ cup chopped nuts

1. Heat oven to 350°F. Grease and flour bottom only of 9 × 5-inch loaf pan. In small bowl, beat cream cheese until light and fluffy. Add 1 egg; blend well. Set aside.
2. In large bowl, combine flour, sugar, baking powder, baking soda and salt; mix well. Stir in apple juice, margarine and beaten egg until well blended. Fold in cranberries and nuts. Spoon half of batter into greased and floured pan. Spoon cream cheese mixture evenly over batter. Top with remaining batter.
3. Bake at 350°F. for 65 to 75 minutes or until top springs back when touched lightly in center. Cool 15 minutes; remove from pan. Cool 1 hour or until completely cooled. Wrap tightly and store in refrigerator.

Yield: 1 (16-slice) loaf
High Altitude (Above 3,500 Feet): Increase flour to 2 cups plus 3 tablespoons; decrease sugar to ½ cup. Bake at 375°F. for 55 to 65 minutes.

Tip: *To chop cranberries in food processor, add about 2 cups fresh cranberries to food processor bowl with metal blade. Process with 10 on/off pulses or until all berries are coarsely chopped.

Nutrition Information Per Serving

Serving Size: 1 Slice. Calories 220 • Calories from Fat 90 • Total Fat 10 g • Saturated Fat 3 g • Cholesterol 40 mg • Sodium 230 mg • Dietary Fiber 1 g
Dietary Exchanges: 2 Starch, 1½ Fat OR 2 Carbohydrate, 1½ Fat

Cider Pumpkin Bread

Prep Time: 15 minutes
(Ready in 2 hours 30 minutes)

1 cup firmly packed brown
sugar
1 cup canned pumpkin
½ cup oil
½ cup apple cider or apple
juice
1 egg

1¾ cups all-purpose flour
½ cup whole wheat flour
3 teaspoons baking powder
1½ teaspoons cinnamon
½ cup chopped nuts
½ cup raisins

1. Heat oven to 350°F. Grease and flour bottom only of
9 × 5-inch loaf pan. In large bowl, combine brown sugar,
pumpkin, oil, apple cider and egg; mix well.
2. Add all-purpose flour, whole wheat flour, baking powder and cinnamon; stir just until dry ingredients are
moistened. Stir in nuts and raisins. Pour into greased
and floured pan.
3. Bake at 350°F. for 55 to 65 minutes or until toothpick
inserted in center comes out clean. Cool 10 minutes;
remove from pan. Cool 1 hour or until completely cooled.
Wrap tightly and store in refrigerator.

Yield: 1 (16-slice) loaf
High Altitude (Above 3,500 Feet): No change.

Nutrition Information Per Serving

Serving Size: 1 Slice. Calories 230 • Calories from Fat 90 • Total Fat 10 g •
Saturated Fat 1 g • Cholesterol 15 mg • Sodium 105 mg • Dietary Fiber 2 g
Dietary Exchanges: 1 Starch, 1 Fruit, 2 Fat OR 2 Carbohydrate, 2 Fat

---

Recipe Variation

Make the bread with
1 cup applesauce or
pureed butternut squash
in place of the pumpkin.

Healthy Hint

Apple cider, made with
fresh apples, is darker in
color and fuller in flavor
than apple juice, which is
generally more processed.
Play it safe, however, and
purchase apple cider
that's been pasteurized to
avoid contamination.

Make It Special

For a holiday hostess gift,
pair this pumpkin bread
with a jug of fresh apple
cider and a packet of
sweet mulling spices or
cinnamon sticks.

Pecan Pumpkin Bread

Recipe Fact

This sweetly spiced harvest quick bread makes two loaves, one for you and one to share. Or, divided into three smaller bread pans, the batter yields three loaves.

Menu Suggestion

Add this loaf, rich with the flavors of autumn, to your Thanksgiving menu. Use it as a sweet pre-dinner nibble or an informal accompaniment for coffee later in the day.

Prep Time: 15 minutes
(Ready in 1 hour 35 minutes)

2½ cups all-purpose flour	1 teaspoon nutmeg
1 cup whole wheat flour	1 cup oil
3 cups sugar	⅔ cup water
2 teaspoons baking soda	4 eggs
1½ teaspoons salt	1 (16-oz.) can (2 cups) pumpkin
2 teaspoons cinnamon	1 cup chopped pecans

1. Heat oven to 350°F. Grease bottom only of two 9 × 5-inch loaf pans or three 8 × 4-inch loaf pans. In large bowl, combine all-purpose flour, whole wheat flour, sugar, baking soda, salt, cinnamon and nutmeg; mix well.

2. In medium bowl, combine oil, water, eggs and pumpkin; blend well. Add to flour mixture; beat 1 minute at medium speed. Fold in pecans. Pour batter into greased pans.

3. Bake at 350°F. for 60 to 70 minutes or until toothpick inserted in center comes out clean. Cool 10 minutes; remove from pans. Cool 1 hour or until completely cooled. Wrap tightly and store in refrigerator.

Yield: 2 (16-slice) loaves
High Altitude (Above 3,500 Feet): No change.

Nutrition Information Per Serving

Serving Size: 1 Slice. Calories 230 • Calories from Fat 90 • Total Fat 10 g •
Saturated Fat 1 g • Cholesterol 25 mg • Sodium 190 mg • Dietary Fiber 2 g
Dietary Exchanges: 1 Starch, 1 Fruit, 2 Fat OR 2 Carbohydrate, 2 Fat

Toasted Pecan and Rhubarb Bread

Prep Time: 15 minutes
(Ready in 2 hours 30 minutes)

¾ cup sugar
½ cup margarine or butter, softened
2 eggs
1 cup buttermilk*
2 cups all-purpose flour

½ cup chopped pecans, toasted**
½ teaspoon baking powder
½ teaspoon baking soda
¼ teaspoon salt
1 cup chopped rhubarb
1 tablespoon sugar

1. Heat oven to 350°F. Grease bottom only of 9 × 5 or 8 × 4-inch loaf pan. In large bowl, combine ¾ cup sugar and margarine; beat until light and fluffy. Add eggs; beat well. Add buttermilk; blend well.

2. In small bowl, combine flour, pecans, baking powder, baking soda and salt; mix well. Add to buttermilk mixture; stir just until dry ingredients are moistened. Fold in rhubarb. Pour batter into greased pan. Sprinkle 1 tablespoon sugar over top.

3. Bake at 350°F. for 50 to 60 minutes or until toothpick inserted in center comes out clean. Cool 15 minutes; remove from pan. Cool 1 hour or until completely cooled. Wrap tightly and store in refrigerator.

Yield: 1 (16-slice) loaf
High Altitude (Above 3,500 Feet): No change.

Tip: *To substitute for buttermilk, use 1 tablespoon vinegar or lemon juice plus milk to make 1 cup.

**To toast pecans, spread on cookie sheet; bake at 350°F. for 5 to 7 minutes or until golden brown, stirring occasionally.

Nutrition Information Per Serving

Serving Size: 1 Slice. Calories 190 • Calories from Fat 80 • Total Fat 9 g •
Saturated Fat 2 g • Cholesterol 25 mg • Sodium 180 mg • Dietary Fiber 1 g
Dietary Exchanges: 1 Starch, ½ Fruit, 2 Fat OR 1½ Carbohydrate, 2 Fat

---

About Rhubarb

Rhubarb is a hardy garden perennial with beautiful glossy green leaves that are actually toxic: only the stalks are edible. In springtime, rhubarb stalks are greenish red and somewhat stringy, sort of like celery but with an unmistakable sour tang. To prepare rhubarb, discard the leaves, then trim the ends of the stalks before chopping. To offset the mouth-puckering flavor, rhubarb is often teamed with a sweet ingredient, such as strawberries.

Menu Suggestion

Serve the bread for breakfast, spread with whipped cream cheese or strawberry jam. Or, transform it into a memorable "shortcake": top with a scoop of vanilla ice cream, sliced fresh strawberries and a dollop of fresh whipped cream.

Pineapple-Zucchini Bread

Recipe Fact

This pretty loaf, with its shimmering glaze, makes a beautiful gift or a special treat for family or guests. Those who don't like vegetables can be told that this is "spice bread"; they'll never guess it's made with shredded zucchini.

Make It Special

Before the glaze has set, decorate the top of the loaf with candied cherry halves and/or nutmeats.

About Canned Pineapple

Canned pineapple is generally available in three forms: crushed (shredded), chunks or rings. It comes packed in its own juices or sweetened.

Prep Time: 25 minutes
(Ready in 2 hours 45 minutes)

Bread
1 cup firmly packed brown sugar
½ cup margarine or butter, softened
1 cup shredded unpeeled zucchini
1 (8-oz.) can crushed pineapple in unsweetened juice, undrained, reserving 1 tablespoon liquid
2 eggs, slightly beaten
2 cups all-purpose flour
1 teaspoon baking soda
1 teaspoon cinnamon
¼ teaspoon salt
¼ teaspoon allspice
½ cup chopped nuts

Glaze
½ cup powdered sugar
1 tablespoon reserved pineapple liquid
1 teaspoon corn syrup
¼ teaspoon cinnamon

1. Heat oven to 350°F. Grease and flour bottom only of 9 × 5-inch loaf pan. In large bowl, combine brown sugar and margarine; beat until light and fluffy. Stir in zucchini, pineapple and eggs.
2. Add flour, baking soda, 1 teaspoon cinnamon, salt and allspice; mix well. Fold in nuts. Spread evenly in greased and floured pan.
3. Bake at 350°F. for 60 to 70 minutes or until toothpick inserted in center comes out clean. Cool 10 minutes; remove from pan.
4. In small bowl, combine all glaze ingredients; beat until smooth. Spoon over warm loaf. Cool 1 hour or until completely cooled. Wrap tightly and store in refrigerator.

Yield: 1 (16-slice) loaf
High Altitude (Above 3,500 Feet): Bake at 375°F. for 55 to 65 minutes.

Nutrition Information Per Serving
Serving Size: 1 Slice. Calories 220 • Calories from Fat 80 • Total Fat 9 g • Saturated Fat 1 g • Cholesterol 25 mg • Sodium 190 mg • Dietary Fiber 1 g Dietary Exchanges: 1 Starch, 1 Fruit, 2 Fat OR 2 Carbohydrate, 2 Fat

Pineapple-Zucchini Bread

Zucchini-Orange Bread

gift idea

Prep Time: 25 minutes
(Ready in 2 hours 30 minutes)

Bread
4 eggs
1½ cups sugar
¾ cup oil
⅔ cup orange juice
2 cups shredded unpeeled
   zucchini
3¼ cups all-purpose flour
1½ teaspoons baking powder
1½ teaspoons baking soda
1 teaspoon salt
2½ teaspoons cinnamon
½ teaspoon cloves
2 teaspoons grated orange
   peel
½ cup chopped nuts, if desired

Glaze
1 cup powdered sugar
2 to 3 teaspoons orange juice

Recipe Fact

Here's a valuable addition to the repertoire of home gardeners (or neighbors of home gardeners) who find themselves with a sudden abundance of overgrown zucchini.

Storage Tip

Freeze the loaf unglazed and glaze it just before serving.

1. Heat oven to 350°F. Grease and flour bottoms only of two 8×4 or 9×5-inch loaf pans. In large bowl, beat eggs until thick and lemon-colored. Gradually beat in sugar. Stir in oil, ⅔ cup orange juice and zucchini until well blended.

2. Add all remaining bread ingredients; mix well. Pour batter into greased and floured pans.

3. Bake at 350°F. for 45 to 55 minutes or until toothpick inserted in center comes out clean. Cool 10 minutes; remove from pans. Cool 15 minutes.

4. In small bowl, combine glaze ingredients, adding enough orange juice for desired spreading consistency. Spread over warm loaves. Cool 45 minutes or until completely cooled. Wrap tightly and store in refrigerator.

Yield: 2 (16-slice) loaves
High Altitude (Above 3,500 Feet): Increase flour to 3¼ cups plus 3 tablespoons.
Bake at 350°F. for 45 to 50 minutes.

Nutrition Information Per Serving
Serving Size: 1 Slice. Calories 170 • Calories from Fat 60 • Total Fat 7 g • Saturated Fat 1 g • Cholesterol 25 mg • Sodium 160 mg • Dietary Fiber 1 g Dietary Exchanges: 1 Starch, ½ Fruit, 1½ Fat OR 1½ Carbohydrate, 1½ Fat

---

Zucchini-Orange Bread

Zucchini Bread with Dried Cranberries

Ingredient Substitution

Raisins, currants or dried cherries may be substituted for the dried cranberries.

Storage Tip

To retain maximum flavor in frozen breads, wrap them tightly in plastic wrap, then double the protection by putting the wrapped loaves into resealable plastic freezer bags. Or, wrap individual slices before freezing, to make it easy to thaw them quickly in the microwave for an afternoon snack or a quick treat when visitors drop by.

Prep Time: 15 minutes
(Ready in 35 minutes)

½ cup sugar
½ cup shredded unpeeled
   zucchini
⅓ cup milk
1 tablespoon oil
1 egg
1 cup all-purpose flour

2 teaspoons baking powder
½ teaspoon cinnamon
¼ teaspoon cloves
½ cup sweetened dried
   cranberries
1 tablespoon sugar, if desired

1. Heat oven to 400°F. Spray 8 or 9-inch round cake pan with nonstick cooking spray.
2. In large bowl, combine ½ cup sugar, zucchini, milk, oil and egg; mix well. Add flour, baking powder, cinnamon, cloves and dried cranberries; mix just until combined. Pour into sprayed pan. Sprinkle with 1 tablespoon sugar.
3. Bake at 400°F. for 12 to 19 minutes or until light golden brown. Cool 5 minutes. Cut into wedges. Serve warm.

Yield: 12 servings
High Altitude (Above 3,500 Feet): No change.

Nutrition Information Per Serving

Serving Size: ¹⁄₁₂ of Recipe. Calories 120 • Calories from Fat 20 • Total Fat 2 g • Saturated Fat 0 g • Cholesterol 20 mg • Sodium 90 mg • Dietary Fiber 1 g
Dietary Exchanges: 1 Starch, ½ Fruit OR 1½ Carbohydrate

Orange-Carrot Bread

Prep Time: 20 minutes
(Ready in 40 minutes)

Bread
3/4 cup finely shredded carrots
1/2 cup sugar
1/4 cup orange juice
1 tablespoon oil
1 egg or 2 egg whites
3/4 cup all-purpose flour
2 teaspoons baking powder

Topping
2 tablespoons sugar
1 tablespoon grated orange
   peel

1. Heat oven to 400°F. Spray 8 or 9-inch round cake pan with nonstick cooking spray. In large bowl, combine carrots, 1/2 cup sugar, orange juice, oil and egg; mix well.
2. Add flour and baking powder; stir just until combined. Pour into sprayed pan.
3. In small bowl, combine topping ingredients; mix well. Sprinkle evenly over batter.
4. Bake at 400°F. for 14 to 19 minutes or until bread is golden brown and springs back when touched lightly in center. Cut into wedges. Serve warm or cool.

Yield: 12 servings
High Altitude (Above 3,500 Feet): Increase flour to 1 cup. Bake as directed above.

Nutrition Information Per Serving
Serving Size: 1/12 of Recipe. Calories 90 • Calories from Fat 20 • Total Fat 2 g • Saturated Fat 0 g • Cholesterol 20 mg • Sodium 90 mg • Dietary Fiber 0 g
Dietary Exchanges: 1 Starch OR 1 Carbohydrate

Kitchen Tip

For baking, use corn oil, canola oil or another neutral-flavored vegetable oil rather than the overly assertive olive oil.

Make It Special

To transform an ordinary paper plate into a pretty dish for gift giving, cover the paper with a piece of holiday wrapping paper cut to size or a lacy paper doily. Cover the plate with plastic wrap so the design shows through but doesn't get stained by the bread.

Menu Suggestion

This lightly sweet bread makes a nice brunch accompaniment for scrambled eggs and fresh fruit.

Banana-Blueberry Mini-Loaves

Prep Time: 15 minutes
(Ready in 1 hour 40 minutes)

1 cup sugar
½ cup oil
1 cup (2 medium) mashed ripe
    bananas
½ cup low-fat plain yogurt
1 teaspoon vanilla

2 eggs
2 cups all-purpose flour
1 teaspoon baking soda
½ teaspoon salt
1 cup fresh or frozen
    blueberries (do not thaw)

1. Heat oven to 350°F. Grease and flour bottoms only of three 6 × 3½-inch loaf pans.* In large bowl, combine sugar and oil; beat well. Add bananas, yogurt, vanilla and eggs; blend well.

2. Add flour, baking soda and salt; stir just until dry ingredients are moistened. Gently stir in blueberries. Pour into greased and floured pans.

3. Bake at 350°F. for 40 to 50 minutes or until toothpick inserted in center comes out clean. Cool 5 minutes; remove from pans. Cool 30 minutes or until completely cooled. Wrap tightly and store in refrigerator.

Yield: 3 (12-slice) loaves

High Altitude (Above 3,500 Feet): Increase flour to 2¼ cups. Bake 6 × 3½-inch pans at 375°F. for 30 to 40 minutes. Bake 9 × 5-inch pan at 375°F. for 50 to 60 minutes.

Tip: *If desired, recipe can be baked in one 9 × 5-inch loaf pan. Grease and flour bottom only of pan. Bake at 350°F. for 60 to 70 minutes.

Nutrition Information Per Serving

Serving Size: 1 Slice. Calories 80 • Calories from Fat 25 • Total Fat 3 g •
Saturated Fat 1 g • Cholesterol 10 mg • Sodium 70 mg • Dietary Fiber 0g
Dietary Exchanges: ½ Starch, ½ Fruit, ½ Fat OR 1 Carbohydrate, ½ Fat

---

low-fat • gift idea

Kitchen Tip

For convenience, bake the loaves in disposable foil mini-loaf pans (available in supermarkets); the pans also make handy "wrappers" for giving loaves to friends.

Ingredient Substitution

Try ½ cup applesauce in place of the yogurt. Like yogurt, applesauce contributes moisture and enhances tenderness, but it also deepens the flavor a bit.

Recipe Variation

Spice up the loaf with 1 teaspoon ground cinnamon and ½ teaspoon ground nutmeg.

Banana-Blueberry Mini-Loaves

Sweet Potato Quick Bread

Kitchen Tip

Mash canned sweet potatoes with a fork or potato masher. Don't worry if there are still a few lumps; the results will still be delicious.

Menu Suggestion

Serve this spiced bread with roasted pork tenderloin, steamed snow peas and wild rice pilaf.

Prep Time: 20 minutes
(Ready in 2 hours 45 minutes)

2$\frac{1}{3}$ cups sugar
$\frac{2}{3}$ cup water
$\frac{2}{3}$ cup oil
4 eggs, beaten
1 (23-oz.) can sweet potatoes
    in syrup, drained, mashed
    (2 cups)

3$\frac{1}{3}$ cups all-purpose flour
2 teaspoons baking soda
1$\frac{1}{2}$ teaspoons salt
1 teaspoon cinnamon
$\frac{1}{2}$ teaspoon baking powder
1 cup chopped pecans,
    if desired

1. Heat oven to 350°F. Grease and flour two 8 × 4 or 9 × 5-inch loaf pans. In large bowl, combine sugar, water, oil, eggs and sweet potatoes; blend well.

2. In medium bowl, combine flour, baking soda, salt, cinnamon and baking powder; mix well. Add to sweet potato mixture; stir just until dry ingredients are moistened. Stir in pecans. Pour into greased and floured pans.

3. Bake at 350°F. for 60 to 70 minutes or until toothpick inserted in center comes out clean. Cool 15 minutes; remove from pans. Cool 1 hour or until completely cooled. Wrap tightly and store in refrigerator.

Yield: 2 (12-slice) loaves
High Altitude (Above 3,500 Feet): Decrease sugar to 2 cups. Bake as directed above.

Nutrition Information Per Serving

Serving Size: 1 Slice. Calories 270 • Calories from Fat 90 • Total Fat 10 g • Saturated Fat 1 g • Cholesterol 35 mg • Sodium 270 mg • Dietary Fiber 2 g Dietary Exchanges: 1½ Starch, 1 Fruit, 2 Fat OR 2½ Carbohydrate, 2 Fat

Sweet Potato Quick Bread

Spicy Sweet Potato Bread

Ingredient Substitution

Use ½ cup dried raisins, dried cranberries or chopped dried apples in place of the currants.

Recipe Variation

Make the loaf with ½ cup canned or cooked pumpkin puree or applesauce instead of the sweet potatoes.

Prep Time: 30 minutes

½ cup sugar
½ cup mashed canned or
   cooked sweet potatoes
⅓ cup milk
1 tablespoon oil
1 egg

1 cup all-purpose flour
2 teaspoons baking powder
¼ teaspoon nutmeg
¼ teaspoon allspice
½ cup dried currants

1. Heat oven to 400°F. Spray 8 or 9-inch square pan with nonstick cooking spray.

2. In large bowl, combine sugar and sweet potatoes; blend well. Add milk, oil and egg; mix well. Add flour, baking powder, nutmeg and allspice; stir just until dry ingredients are moistened. Stir in currants. Pour batter into sprayed pan.

3. Bake at 400°F. for 12 to 19 minutes or until bread is light golden brown and center is firm to the touch. Cut into squares. Serve warm or cool.

Yield: 12 servings
High Altitude (Above 3,500 Feet): No change.

Nutrition Information Per Serving

Serving Size: 1/12 of Recipe. Calories 120 • Calories from Fat 20 • Total Fat 2 g • Saturated Fat 0 g • Cholesterol 20 mg • Sodium 95 mg • Dietary Fiber 1 g Dietary Exchanges: 1 Starch, ½ Fruit OR 1½ Carbohydrate

Tomato-Basil Dinner Bread

Prep Time: 10 minutes
(Ready in 40 minutes)

2 cups all-purpose flour
1½ teaspoons baking powder
½ teaspoon baking soda
¼ teaspoon salt
1 cup (3 medium) chopped
   Italian plum tomatoes

¾ cup plain yogurt
¼ cup chopped fresh basil
2 tablespoons margarine or
   butter, softened
1 egg

1. Heat oven to 400°F. Spray 9-inch round cake pan with nonstick cooking spray. In large bowl, combine flour, baking powder, baking soda and salt; mix well.

2. In small bowl, combine tomatoes, yogurt, basil, margarine and egg; blend well. Add to flour mixture; stir just until dry ingredients are moistened. Spoon dough evenly into sprayed pan.

3. Bake at 400°F. for 22 to 28 minutes or until bread is golden brown and center is firm to the touch. Cut into wedges. Serve warm.

Yield: 12 servings
High Altitude (Above 3,500 Feet): No change.

Nutrition Information Per Serving
Serving Size: ¹⁄₁₂ of Recipe. Calories 120 • Calories from Fat 25 • Total Fat 3 g •
Saturated Fat 1 g • Cholesterol 20 mg • Sodium 200 mg • Dietary Fiber 1 g
Dietary Exchanges: 1 Starch, ½ Fat OR 1 Carbohydrate, ½ Fat

Menu Suggestion

Fresh basil and fresh tomatoes: This is the perfect bread for summer. It goes perfectly with any kind of grilled poultry or fish. Make a colorful salad of black beans, fresh cooked corn-on-the-cob kernels, chopped green onion and parsley, all tossed with red wine vinaigrette.

Classic Cornbread

Prep Time: 10 minutes
(Ready in 35 minutes)

Kitchen Tip

Cornbread stick pans have individual compartments to make "sticks" (elongated muffins) shaped like ears of corn. Traditional pans are made of cast iron and, like other cast-iron cookware, benefit from being "seasoned" (heat, wipe with vegetable oil, cool and repeat) before initial use and after each subsequent use. Over time, cast iron builds up an almost non-stick surface. Wash with hot water and a plastic scrubber but not steel wool or soap, which removes the seasoning.

About Cornmeal

Cornmeal, which is ground from dried corn kernels, is a staple in many international cuisines. In Italy, it's mixed with liquid to form polenta, a cornmeal mush. In Mexico, traditional home cooks and commercial bakeries make tortillas and tamales out of cornmeal.

1 cup all-purpose flour
1 cup cornmeal
2 tablespoons sugar
3 teaspoons baking powder

½ teaspoon salt
1 cup milk
¼ cup oil or melted shortening
1 egg, slightly beaten

1. Heat oven to 425°F. Grease 8 or 9-inch square pan. In medium bowl, combine flour, cornmeal, sugar, baking powder and salt; mix well. Stir in all remaining ingredients just until smooth. Pour batter into greased pan.
2. Bake at 425°F. for 18 to 22 minutes or until toothpick inserted in center comes out clean. Cut into squares. Serve warm.

Yield: 9 servings
High Altitude (Above 3,500 Feet): Decrease baking powder to 2 teaspoons.
Bake as directed above.

Nutrition Information Per Serving
Serving Size: ⅑ of Recipe. Calories 190 • Calories from Fat 70 • Total Fat 8 g • Saturated Fat 1 g • Cholesterol 25 mg • Sodium 310 mg • Dietary Fiber 1 g
Dietary Exchanges: 1½ Starch, 1½ Fat OR 1½ Carbohydrate, 1½ Fat

Variations

Bacon Cornbread: Cook 4 to 5 slices bacon until crisp; drain on paper towel. Substitute bacon drippings for oil. Sprinkle batter with crumbled bacon before baking.

Cornbread Muffins: Spoon batter into greased muffin cups. Bake 15 to 20 minutes. Immediately remove from muffin cups. Yield: 12 muffins

Cornbread Ring: Spoon batter into greased 1½-quart (6-cup) ring mold. Bake 15 to 20 minutes. Immediately remove from mold.

Cornbread Sticks: Spoon batter into well-greased, hot corn stick pan, filling ⅔ full. Bake 12 to 15 minutes. Immediately remove from pan. Yield: 18 corn sticks

Mexican Cornbread

Prep Time: 15 minutes
(Ready in 1 hour 15 minutes)

6 oz. (1½ cups) shredded
    sharp Cheddar cheese
¾ cup buttermilk*
⅓ cup oil
2 eggs, slightly beaten
1 (8.5-oz.) can cream-style corn

1 (4-oz.) can chopped green
    chiles
1 cup cornmeal
1 cup all-purpose flour
1 teaspoon baking powder
½ teaspoon baking soda
½ teaspoon salt

1. Heat oven to 375°F. Generously grease 1½-quart casserole. In large bowl, combine cheese, buttermilk, oil, eggs, corn and chiles; blend well.

2. In small bowl, combine cornmeal, flour, baking powder, baking soda and salt; mix well. Add to cheese mixture; stir just until dry ingredients are moistened. Pour into greased casserole.

3. Bake at 375°F. for 40 to 50 minutes or until cornbread is deep golden brown and toothpick inserted in center comes out clean. Cool 10 minutes; remove from casserole. Serve warm.

Yield: 12 servings
High Altitude (Above 3,500 Feet): No change.

Tip: *To substitute for buttermilk, use 2 teaspoons vinegar or lemon juice plus milk to make ¾ cup.

Nutrition Information Per Serving

Serving Size: ¹⁄₁₂ of Recipe. Calories 220 • Calories from Fat 110 • Total Fat 12 g • Saturated Fat 4 g • Cholesterol 50 mg • Sodium 370 mg • Dietary Fiber 2 g Dietary Exchanges: 1 Starch, 1 Vegetable, ½ High-Fat Meat, 1½ Fat OR 1 Carbohydrate, 1 Vegetable, ½ High-Fat Meat, 1½ Fat

---

Ingredient Substitution

You may use 1 cup left-over cooked fresh corn kernels in place of the canned corn.

Menu Suggestion

Serve this zesty cornbread with chili or a spicy meat stew, tossed salad and iced tea or Mexican beer.

Mexican Cornbread

Southwest Salsa Cornbread

Prep Time: 10 minutes
(Ready in 35 minutes)

1¼ cups all-purpose flour
¾ cup cornmeal
2 teaspoons baking powder
¼ teaspoon salt
1 cup frozen whole kernel corn
    or 7-oz. can vacuum-packed
    whole kernel corn, drained

¾ cup skim milk
½ cup chunky style salsa
3 tablespoons oil
1 egg

1. Heat oven to 400°F. Spray 9-inch square pan with non-stick cooking spray.
2. In large bowl, combine flour, cornmeal, baking powder and salt; mix well. Add all remaining ingredients; stir just until dry ingredients are moistened. Spoon batter evenly into sprayed pan.
3. Bake at 400°F. for 18 to 23 minutes or until toothpick inserted in center comes out clean. Cut into squares. Serve warm.

Yield: 12 servings
High Altitude (Above 3,500 Feet): No change.

Nutrition Information Per Serving
Serving Size: ¹⁄₁₂ of Recipe. Calories 130 • Calories from Fat 35 • Total Fat 4 g • Saturated Fat 1 g • Cholesterol 20 mg • Sodium 220 mg • Dietary Fiber 1 g Dietary Exchanges: 1½ Starch, ½ Fat OR 1½ Carbohydrate, ½ Fat

About Southwest Flavors

In recent years, the rest of the United States has discovered the wonderful flavors long favored by people in Santa Fe, Albuquerque and other parts of the American Southwest. Typical ingredients show Mexican influence and include corn or cornmeal, tortillas and tortilla chips, tomatoes and tomato concoctions such as salsa, assertive seasonings such as cilantro and cumin, and all manner of peppers, including sweet bell and numerous types of mild and hot chile peppers.

Menu Suggestion

Serve the bread alongside grilled chicken breasts and grilled zucchini. Make a salad of black beans and garbanzos tossed with cilantro vinaigrette. For dessert, serve flan, the simple yet exquisitely delicious silken caramel custard that's a favorite in Spain and all over Latin America.

Salsa Bread Olé

gift idea

Prep Time: 30 minutes
(Ready in 1 hour 55 minutes)

3 eggs
½ cup cornmeal
⅔ cup buttermilk*
½ cup butter, softened
1 (16-oz.) jar chunky style
    salsa, well drained
½ cup chopped ripe olives
¼ cup chopped scallions or
    green onions
1 tablespoon chopped fresh
    parsley
5 oz. (1¼ cups) shredded
    Cheddar cheese

1 oz. (¼ cup) shredded
    Monterey Jack cheese, if
    desired
2 cups all-purpose flour
1 cup mashed potato flakes
4 teaspoons taco seasoning
    mix (from 1¼-oz. pkg.)
3 teaspoons baking powder
1 teaspoon baking soda
¼ teaspoon salt
¼ teaspoon pepper

1. Heat oven to 350°F. Grease and flour 10-inch tube or 12-cup Bundt pan. In large bowl, beat eggs at high speed for 1 minute. Add cornmeal, buttermilk, butter and salsa; beat 1 minute at medium speed or until well blended. With spoon, stir in olives, scallions, parsley and cheeses.
2. In medium bowl, combine all remaining ingredients; mix well. Add to salsa mixture. Stir just until dry ingredients are moistened. Spoon batter into greased and floured pan.
3. Bake at 350°F. for 45 to 50 minutes or until toothpick inserted in center comes out clean. Cool 15 minutes; remove from pan. Cool on wire rack for 20 minutes. Serve warm.

Yield: 1 (24-slice) loaf
High Altitude (Above 3,500 Feet): No change.

Tip: *To substitute for buttermilk, use 2 teaspoons vinegar or lemon juice plus milk to make ⅔ cup.

Nutrition Information Per Serving
Serving Size: 1 Slice. Calories 140 • Calories from Fat 60 • Total Fat 7 g •
Saturated Fat 4 g • Cholesterol 45 mg • Sodium 360 mg • Dietary Fiber 1 g
Dietary Exchanges: 1 Starch, 1½ Fat OR 1 Carbohydrate, 1½ Fat
---

About Salsa

Marketing statistics indicate that salsa has become America's favorite condiment, surpassing even ketchup and mustard. Salsa, which is Spanish for "sauce," consists of any combination of minced vegetables and seasonings intended to be served as a condiment or dip. The most popular varieties are made with chopped tomato, onion, peppers and fresh cilantro. Intensity can range from mild to fiery.

Menu Suggestion

This hearty bread, flecked with vegetables and cheese, is practically a meal in itself. Serve it with pork strips pan-fried with onions and seasoned with salt, pepper and cumin or chili powder. Make a salad of cherry tomato halves, chopped cucumber and minced red onion tossed with parsley vinaigrette.

Cheddar-Pepper Cornbread

Prep Time: 15 minutes
(Ready in 40 minutes)

1 cup all-purpose flour
1 cup yellow cornmeal
3 teaspoons baking powder
½ teaspoon salt
½ teaspoon cumin
1 cup skim milk
¼ cup honey

¼ cup nonfat plain yogurt
3 egg whites
½ cup chopped red bell
pepper
4 oz. (1 cup) shredded Cheddar
cheese

1. Heat oven to 425°F. Spray 9-inch square pan with non-stick cooking spray. In large bowl, combine flour, cornmeal, baking powder, salt and cumin; mix well.
2. In medium bowl, combine milk, honey, yogurt and egg whites; blend well. Stir in bell pepper and ½ cup of the cheese. Add to flour mixture; stir just until dry ingredients are moistened. (Batter will be lumpy.) Pour into sprayed pan. Sprinkle with remaining ½ cup cheese.
3. Bake at 425°F. for 18 to 22 minutes or until toothpick inserted in center comes out clean. Cut into squares. Serve warm.

Yield: 12 servings
High Altitude (Above 3,500 Feet): No change.

Nutrition Information Per Serving
Serving Size: 1/12 of Recipe. Calories 160 • Calories from Fat 35 • Total Fat 4 g • Saturated Fat 2 g • Cholesterol 10 mg • Sodium 300 mg • Dietary Fiber 1 g
Dietary Exchanges: 1½ Starch, 1 Fat OR 1½ Carbohydrate, 1 Fat

About Cheddar Cheese

Cheddar cheese, originally from the town of Cheddar in England, is a semi-firm slicing cheese. Depending on how long the cheese is aged, the flavor is classified as mild, sharp or extra-sharp. Cheddar's flavor is assertive without being intensely aromatic or overbearing.

Kitchen Tip

Leftover cornbread can be crumbled and used in place of bread crumbs or oatmeal in your favorite meatloaf, meatballs or poultry dressing.

Menu Suggestion

Serve these savory squares with chili and a tossed salad.

Cheddar-Pepper Cornbread

Quick Cheese and Pepper Bread

Prep Time: 15 minutes
(Ready in 1 hour 15 minutes)

2 cups all-purpose flour
4 oz. (1 cup) shredded sharp or
    medium Cheddar cheese
1 tablespoon sugar
½ teaspoon baking powder
½ teaspoon baking soda
½ teaspoon salt

½ teaspoon coarse ground
    black pepper
1 cup buttermilk*
⅓ cup margarine or butter,
    melted
2 eggs

1. Heat oven to 350°F. Grease bottom only of 9 × 5 or
8 × 4-inch loaf pan. In medium bowl, combine flour,
cheese, sugar, baking powder, baking soda, salt and pepper; mix well.

2. In small bowl, combine buttermilk, margarine and
eggs; blend well. Add to flour mixture; stir just until dry
ingredients are moistened. Pour into greased pan.

3. Bake at 350°F. for 35 to 45 minutes or until toothpick
inserted in center comes out clean. Cool 15 minutes;
remove from pan. Serve warm or cool completely on wire
rack. Wrap tightly and store in refrigerator.

Yield: 1 (16-slice) loaf
High Altitude (Above 3,500 Feet): No change.

Tip: *To substitute for buttermilk, use 1 tablespoon vinegar or lemon
juice plus milk to make 1 cup.

Nutrition Information Per Serving

Serving Size: 1 Slice. Calories 140 • Calories from Fat 60 • Total Fat 7 g •
Saturated Fat 2 g • Cholesterol 35 mg • Sodium 230 mg • Dietary Fiber 0 g
Dietary Exchanges: 1 Starch, 1 Fat OR 1 Carbohydrate, 1 Fat

About Black Pepper

The black peppercorn,
native to Asia, is a type of
berry that's allowed to
dry. As it dries, the berry
changes color from red to
the characteristic black,
shriveled peppercorn.
White pepper, which has a
milder flavor, comes from
the same berry but has
had the outer black part
removed. For freshest
flavor, purchase pepper-
corns whole and grind
them as needed in a
peppermill.

Menu Suggestion

Complement a casserole
meal with this easy loaf of
bread, or serve the bread
with a savory omelet for a
Sunday brunch or infor-
mal supper.

Recipe Variation

Stir ¼ cup minced
pimiento or minced
roasted red bell pepper
into the wet ingredients
before combining them
with the flour mixture.

Quick Cheese and Pepper Bread

Rosemary-Bell Pepper Bread

Prep Time: 10 minutes
(Ready in 35 minutes)

About Bell Peppers

All bell peppers are green when immature. When ripe, peppers become red, yellow or even purple, depending on the variety. Green peppers are less perishable and therefore considerably less expensive (usually about half to one-third the price per pound) than the other colors. At the market, choose peppers that are smooth and glossy, without any shriveled skin or soft spots. Store peppers, unwrapped, in the refrigerator's produce drawer.

Menu Suggestion

For a delicious spring-time menu, serve this bread with roasted chicken, steamed fresh asparagus and a dessert of fresh strawberries and whipped cream.

$1\frac{3}{4}$ cups all-purpose flour
$1\frac{1}{2}$ teaspoons baking powder
$\frac{1}{2}$ teaspoon baking soda
$\frac{1}{4}$ teaspoon salt
2 tablespoons margarine or butter
$\frac{2}{3}$ cup skim milk
$\frac{1}{2}$ cup chopped red, yellow or green bell pepper

1 teaspoon chopped fresh rosemary or $\frac{1}{2}$ teaspoon dried rosemary leaves, crushed
1 egg or 2 egg whites
2 tablespoons grated Parmesan cheese

1. Heat oven to 400°F. Spray 8 or 9-inch round cake pan with nonstick cooking spray. In large bowl, combine flour, baking powder, baking soda and salt; mix well. With pastry blender or fork, cut in margarine until well mixed.
2. Stir in milk, bell pepper, rosemary and egg until soft dough forms. Spread dough evenly in sprayed pan. Sprinkle with Parmesan cheese.
3. Bake at 400°F. for 16 to 22 minutes or until center is firm to the touch and cheese is golden brown. Cut into wedges. Serve warm or cool.

Yield: 12 servings
High Altitude (Above 3,500 Feet): No change.

Nutrition Information Per Serving
Serving Size: $\frac{1}{12}$ of Recipe. Calories 100 • Calories from Fat 25 • Total Fat 3 g •
Saturated Fat 1 g • Cholesterol 20 mg • Sodium 210 mg • Dietary Fiber 1 g
Dietary Exchanges: 1 Starch, $\frac{1}{2}$ Fat OR 1 Carbohydrate, $\frac{1}{2}$ Fat

Top to bottom: Rosemary-Bell Pepper Bread; Southwest Salsa Cornbread, page 178; Zucchini Bread with Dried Cranberries, page 166

Zucchini-Cheese Bread

Prep Time: 25 minutes
(Ready in 1 hour 5 minutes)

Recipe Fact

This colorful wholesome bread is chock-full of good things. Using low-fat yogurt instead of oil reduces the fat considerably. The Swiss and Parmesan cheeses add calcium, riboflavin (vitamin B₂) and a bit of protein.

About Pimientos

Pimientos, more often sold in jars than fresh, come from a particularly thick-skinned sweet pepper that looks like a heart-shaped bell pepper.

Menu Suggestions

Serve the bread with a fresh fruit salad and cups of piping hot tea with lemon.

For a vegetarian feast, serve this bread alongside a hearty rice-and-bean entree and a large tossed salad.

1 cup all-purpose flour
1 teaspoon baking powder
½ teaspoon onion salt
¼ teaspoon garlic powder
1 cup coarsely shredded unpeeled zucchini
¼ cup plain yogurt

1 (2-oz.) jar chopped pimientos, drained
2 tablespoons grated Parmesan cheese
¼ teaspoon hot pepper sauce
1 egg
1 oz. (¼ cup) shredded Swiss cheese

1. Heat oven to 350°F. Spray 8 or 9-inch round cake pan with nonstick cooking spray. In large bowl, combine flour, baking powder, onion salt and garlic powder; mix well.

2. In medium bowl, combine zucchini, yogurt, pimientos, Parmesan cheese, hot pepper sauce and egg; blend well. Add to flour mixture; stir just until dry ingredients are moistened. Spread batter evenly in sprayed pan.

3. Bake at 350°F. for 30 to 35 minutes or until toothpick inserted in center comes out clean. Sprinkle Swiss cheese over top; bake an additional 2 to 3 minutes or until cheese is melted. Cut into wedges. Serve warm.

Yield: 8 servings
High Altitude (Above 3,500 Feet): No change.

Nutrition Information Per Serving
Serving Size: ⅛ of Recipe. Calories 90 • Calories from Fat 20 • Total Fat 2 g • Saturated Fat 1 g • Cholesterol 30 mg • Sodium 220 mg • Dietary Fiber 1 g
Dietary Exchanges: 1 Starch OR 1 Carbohydrate

Summer Squash Bread with Lemon and Dill

low-fat

Prep Time: 15 minutes
(Ready in 45 minutes)

2½ cups all-purpose flour
2 tablespoons chopped fresh
　dill or 2 teaspoons dried
　dill weed
2 teaspoons grated lemon peel
1 teaspoon baking soda
½ teaspoon baking powder

¼ teaspoon salt
2 tablespoons margarine or
　butter
1 cup skim milk
½ cup finely shredded yellow
　summer squash or zucchini
1 tablespoon skim milk

1. Heat oven to 400°F. Spray cookie sheet with nonstick cooking spray. In large bowl, combine flour, dill, lemon peel, baking soda, baking powder and salt; mix well. With pastry blender or fork, cut in margarine until well mixed.
2. Stir in 1 cup milk and squash until mixture forms a stiff dough. With sprayed hands, shape dough into 7-inch round on sprayed cookie sheet. Brush top with 1 tablespoon milk.
3. Bake at 400°F. for 20 to 30 minutes or until golden brown. Cut into slices. Serve warm or cool.

Yield: 1 (18-slice) loaf
High Altitude (Above 3,500 Feet): No change.

Nutrition Information Per Serving
Serving Size: 1 Slice. Calories 70 • Calories from Fat 10 • Total Fat 1 g •
Saturated Fat 0 g • Cholesterol 0 mg • Sodium 135 mg • Dietary Fiber 1 g
Dietary Exchanges: 1 Starch OR 1 Carbohydrate

Recipe Fact

This savory herbed bread is a variation on a traditional Irish soda bread. It's equally good served warm or at room temperature.

Recipe Variation

Substitute 1 tablespoon minced fresh rosemary (or 1 teaspoon dried) for the dill; add ¼ cup minced oil-cured olives to the dough.

Irish Soda Bread

About Caraway Seed

Caraway seed, traditional in rye bread and Irish soda bread, is a member of the parsley family. (Even "seedless" rye breads often use ground caraway seed as a flavoring.) Central European and Scandinavian cooks use the seeds extensively in dishes made with meat, noodles or cheese.

Kitchen Tip

For an authentic touch, bake the bread in an 8-inch cast-iron frying pan instead of a cake pan.

Menu Suggestion

Irish Soda Bread rounds out a St. Patrick's Day meal of corned beef and cabbage.

Prep Time: 15 minutes
(Ready in 1 hour)

2¼ cups all-purpose flour
2 tablespoons sugar
1 teaspoon baking powder
1 teaspoon baking soda
½ teaspoon salt
¼ cup margarine or butter

½ cup raisins
2 teaspoons caraway seed, if desired
1 cup buttermilk*
1 tablespoon margarine or butter, melted

1. Heat oven to 375°F. Grease 8-inch round cake pan. In large bowl, combine flour, sugar, baking powder, baking soda and salt; blend well. With pastry blender or fork, cut in ¼ cup margarine until mixture is crumbly. Stir in raisins and caraway seed. Add milk all at once; blend well.

2. On well-floured surface, knead dough 5 or 6 times or until no longer sticky. Press dough in greased pan. With sharp knife, cut an "X" ¼ inch deep on top of loaf. Brush with melted margarine.

3. Bake at 375°F. for 25 to 35 minutes or until golden brown. Immediately remove from pan. Cool on wire rack for 10 minutes. Serve warm.

Yield: 1 (16-slice) loaf
High Altitude (Above 3,500 Feet): No change.

Tip: *To substitute for buttermilk, use 1 tablespoon vinegar or lemon juice plus milk to make 1 cup.

Nutrition Information Per Serving

Serving Size: 1 Slice. Calories 130 • Calories from Fat 35 • Total Fat 4 g • Saturated Fat 1 g • Cholesterol 0 mg • Sodium 230 mg • Dietary Fiber 1 g
Dietary Exchanges: 1½ Starch, ½ Fat OR 1½ Carbohydrate, ½ Fat

Whole Wheat Soda Bread

Prep Time: 15 minutes
(Ready in 1 hour)

2 cups whole wheat flour
1 teaspoon baking soda
½ teaspoon salt

1 cup buttermilk*
2 tablespoons honey
1 egg, well beaten

1. Heat oven to 375°F. Grease cookie sheet. In large bowl, combine flour, baking soda and salt; mix well.
2. In small bowl, combine buttermilk, honey and egg; blend well. Add to flour mixture; stir gently just until dry ingredients are moistened. (Dough will be sticky.) Shape dough into flat 7-inch round loaf on greased cookie sheet.
3. Bake at 375°F. for 25 to 30 minutes or until golden brown. Immediately remove from cookie sheet; cool on wire rack for 15 minutes. Serve warm or cool.

Yield: 1 (12-slice) loaf
High Altitude (Above 3,500 Feet): No change.

Tip: *To substitute for buttermilk, use 1 tablespoon vinegar or lemon juice plus milk to make 1 cup.

Nutrition Information Per Serving
Serving Size: 1 Slice. Calories 100 • Calories from Fat 10 • Total Fat 1 g •
Saturated Fat 0 g • Cholesterol 20 mg • Sodium 220 mg • Dietary Fiber 2 g
Dietary Exchanges: 1 Starch OR 1 Carbohydrate

Recipe Variation

Sprinkle the top of the loaf with sesame seed before baking it.

Menu Suggestion

Serve this nutty-textured whole wheat bread with soup and fruit for a casual, satisfying lunch.

Fruited Irish Soda Bread

Prep Time: 15 minutes
(Ready in 1 hour)

2 cups all-purpose flour	¼ teaspoon cinnamon
½ cup whole wheat flour	¼ cup margarine or butter
3 tablespoons brown sugar	1¼ cups buttermilk*
1 teaspoon baking powder	1 cup dried fruit bits
1 teaspoon baking soda	¼ cup candied orange peel,
¼ teaspoon salt	finely chopped

Ingredient Substitution

Personalize the character of this recipe by using your favorite type of dried fruit. Raisins and currants are traditional with soda bread; the candied fruit mixtures typically used for holiday fruit cakes work well, too. For a bit of exotic flair, try chopped dried papaya, mango, pineapple or starfruit. Look for tropical dried fruits in large supermarkets, produce shops or health food stores.

Recipe Variation

Add 1 teaspoon caraway seed to the dough.

Kitchen Tip

For a softer crust, brush the top of the warm loaf with melted butter.

1. Heat oven to 375°F. Lightly grease cookie sheet. In large bowl, combine all-purpose flour, whole wheat flour, brown sugar, baking powder, baking soda, salt and cinnamon; mix well. With fork or pastry blender, cut in margarine until crumbly. Add buttermilk, fruit bits and orange peel; blend well.

2. On well-floured surface, knead dough gently 1 to 2 minutes or until no longer sticky. Form dough into ball; place on greased cookie sheet. With sharp knife, cut an "X" ¼ inch deep on top of loaf.

3. Bake at 375°F. for 40 to 45 minutes or until bread is golden brown and toothpick inserted in center comes out clean. Immediately remove from cookie sheet. Serve warm or cool.

Yield: 1 (16-slice) loaf
High Altitude (Above 3,500 Feet): No change.

Tip: *To substitute for buttermilk, use 4 teaspoons vinegar or lemon juice plus milk to make 1¼ cups.

Nutrition Information Per Serving

Serving Size: 1 Slice. Calories 140 • Calories from Fat 25 • Total Fat 3 g •
Saturated Fat 1 g • Cholesterol 0 mg • Sodium 200 mg • Dietary Fiber 2 g
Dietary Exchanges: 1 Starch, ½ Fruit, ½ Fat OR 1½ Carbohydrate, ½ Fat

Spoon Bread

Prep Time: 25 minutes
(Ready in 1 hour 15 minutes)

2 cups water
1 cup white cornmeal
1 teaspoon seasoned salt
1 cup buttermilk*

2 tablespoons margarine or
  butter, melted
2 teaspoons baking powder
3 eggs, separated

1. Heat oven to 375°F. Grease 2-quart casserole. In medium saucepan, bring water to a boil. Slowly stir in cornmeal and salt. Reduce heat to medium; cook about 5 minutes or until very thick, stirring constantly. Remove from heat; stir in buttermilk. Cool 5 minutes.

2. Gradually beat in 2 tablespoons margarine, baking powder and egg yolks. In small bowl, beat egg whites until stiff but not dry. Fold into cornmeal mixture. Pour batter into greased casserole.

3. Bake at 375°F. for 40 to 50 minutes or until bread is golden brown and knife inserted near center comes out clean. Serve immediately with margarine, if desired.

Yield: 8 (½-cup) servings

Tip: *To substitute for buttermilk, use 1 tablespoon vinegar or lemon juice plus milk to make 1 cup.

Nutrition Information Per Serving

Serving Size: ½ Cup. Calories 130 • Calories from Fat 50 • Total Fat 6 g •
Saturated Fat 1 g • Cholesterol 80 mg • Sodium 410 mg • Dietary Fiber 1 g
Dietary Exchanges: 1 Starch, 1 Fat OR 1 Carbohydrate, 1 Fat

Recipe Fact

Spoon bread, a tradition in the Southeast, is a light, moist cornbread—not quite bread, not quite custard—baked in a casserole and served with a spoon.

Make It Special

Sprinkle a little grated Parmesan cheese over the top of the casserole before baking it.

Menu Suggestion

Serve this with fried chicken (or breaded oven-baked poultry) and coleslaw.

Brown Bread

Prep Time: 20 minutes
(Ready in 2 hours 20 minutes)

Recipe Fact

Brown bread, a.k.a.
Boston bread, is a favorite
companion for Boston
baked beans. It's a sweet
loaf made dark with
molasses and flecked with
raisins. Traditionally,
brown bread was steamed
on the stove-top in a can
or cylindrical pudding
mold. The inclusion of
cornmeal in this recipe
makes the resulting
flavor reminiscent of
Anadama bread, a sweet
yeast bread made with
molasses and cornmeal.

About Buttermilk

Buttermilk is available
fresh in any supermarket;
Southern stores also
carry a powdered version.
Fresh and powdered but-
termilk can be used interchangeably. To substitute
powdered, add the correct
amount of powder with
the dry ingredients, then
stir the corresponding
amount of water into the
wet ingredients.

2 cups raisins
Boiling water
½ cup firmly packed brown
**   sugar**
¼ cup margarine or butter,
**   softened**
1 cup cornmeal
½ cup molasses
2 cups buttermilk*
1 egg
3 cups all-purpose flour
2 teaspoons baking soda

1. Heat oven to 350°F. Grease and flour bottoms only of two 1-quart casseroles or two 8 × 4-inch loaf pans. In small bowl, cover raisins with boiling water; let stand 5 minutes. Drain.

2. In large bowl, combine brown sugar and margarine; beat until light and fluffy. Add cornmeal, molasses, but-termilk and egg; blend well. Stir in flour and baking soda until well mixed. Fold in raisins. Pour batter into greased and floured casseroles.

3. Bake at 350°F. for 40 to 50 minutes or until toothpick inserted in center comes out clean. Cool 10 minutes; remove from casseroles. Cool 1 hour or until completely cooled. Wrap tightly and store in refrigerator.

Yield: 2 (16-slice) loaves
High Altitude (Above 3,500 Feet): No change.

Tip: *To substitute for buttermilk, use 2 tablespoons vinegar or lemon juice plus milk to make 2 cups.

Nutrition Information Per Serving
Serving Size: 1 Slice. Calories 140 • Calories from Fat 20 • Total Fat 2 g •
Saturated Fat 0 g • Cholesterol 5 mg • Sodium 120 mg • Dietary Fiber 1 g
Dietary Exchanges: 1 Starch, 1 Fruit OR 2 Carbohydrate

Brown Bread

Coffee Cakes

Even though most of us don't have the luxury of lolling over coffee and cake on ordinary weekday mornings, coffee cakes are still among the most satisfying of home-baked goods and perfect for leisurely weekend mornings. There's a style for every occasion—from hearty, homestyle cakes for casual get-togethers to elaborate ones with fillings and fancy toppings.

Coffee Cakes

Previous page: Raspberry Cream Cheese Coffee Cake, page 216

Sour Cream Coffee Cake

Prep Time: 25 minutes
(Ready in 1 hour 10 minutes)

Coffee Cake
1 cup butter, softened
1½ cups sugar
3 eggs
1 teaspoon vanilla
3 cups all-purpose flour
2½ teaspoons baking powder
1 teaspoon salt
¼ teaspoon baking soda

1 cup sour cream
½ cup milk

Filling
¼ cup firmly packed brown
  sugar
1 teaspoon cinnamon
½ cup chopped pecans

1. Heat oven to 350°F. Grease and flour 12-cup Bundt® pan or 10-inch tube pan. In large bowl, combine butter and sugar; beat until light and fluffy. Add eggs one at a time, beating well after each addition. Add vanilla; blend well.

2. In large bowl, combine flour, baking powder, salt and baking soda; mix well. Alternately add flour mixture, sour cream and milk to butter mixture, beginning and ending with flour mixture and mixing well after each addition. Spoon half of batter into greased and floured pan.

3. In small bowl, combine all filling ingredients; mix well. Sprinkle mixture evenly over batter in pan. Spoon remaining batter over filling.

4. Bake at 350°F. for 50 to 60 minutes or until toothpick inserted 1 inch from edge comes out clean. Cool in pan 10 minutes; invert onto wire rack. Cool at least 15 minutes. Serve warm or cool.

Yield: 15 servings
High Altitude (Above 3,500 Feet): Decrease sugar to 1¼ cups.
Bake at 350°F. for 55 to 65 minutes.

Recipe Fact
This is the classic: a basic sour cream coffee cake with cinnamon-sugar lacing through the center of the cake and sprinkled on top.

Make It Special
This moist, tender-crumbed cake is a good choice when you need something sweet to take to a friend or neighbor. Wrap the cake in plastic and tuck a small nosegay of flowers into the opening in the center of the ring-shaped cake.

Recipe Variation
Add 1 cup chocolate chips to the filling, or sprinkle a layer of blueberries, raisins, raspberries or shredded apple onto the batter into the center along with the filling mixture.

Nutrition Information Per Serving
Serving Size: ¹⁄₁₅ of Recipe. Calories 380 • Calories from Fat 180 • Total Fat 20 g • Saturated Fat 10 g • Cholesterol 85 mg • Sodium 400 mg • Dietary Fiber 1 g
Dietary Exchanges: 1½ Starch, 1½ Fruit, 4 Fat OR 3 Carbohydrate, 4 Fat

Cinnamon Coffee Cake

Recipe Fact

This moist coffee cake tastes like homemade buttermilk doughnuts rolled in sugar and cinnamon, but it's much easier to make!

Recipe Variation

Press pitted fresh plum halves into the top of the cake and sprinkle with the cinnamon-sugar topping before baking.

Make It Special

For a festive tea party, top squares of cake with a spoonful of whipped cream and fresh raspberries, blueberries or sliced strawberries.

Coffee Cake

1³/₄ cups all-purpose flour
³/₄ cup sugar
2 teaspoons baking powder
¹/₄ teaspoon baking soda
¹/₄ teaspoon salt
¹/₄ teaspoon nutmeg
³/₄ cup buttermilk*

¹/₃ cup margarine or butter, melted
1 teaspoon vanilla
2 eggs, beaten

Topping

¹/₄ cup margarine or butter, melted
3 tablespoons sugar
¹/₂ teaspoon cinnamon

1. Heat oven to 350°F. Grease bottom only of 9-inch square pan. In large bowl, combine all coffee cake ingredients; stir just until dry ingredients are moistened. Spread batter in greased pan.

2. Bake at 350°F. for 30 to 40 minutes or until toothpick inserted in center comes out clean.

3. Generously pierce hot cake with fork. Brush or drizzle ¹/₄ cup melted margarine over hot cake. In small bowl, combine 3 tablespoons sugar and cinnamon; mix well. Sprinkle over hot cake. Serve warm.

Yield: 9 servings
High Altitude (Above 3,500 Feet): Increase flour to 1³/₄ cups plus 2 tablespoons.
Bake as directed above.

Tip: *To substitute for buttermilk, use 2¹/₄ teaspoons vinegar or lemon juice plus milk to make ³/₄ cup.

Nutrition Information Per Serving

Serving Size: ¹/₉ of Recipe. Calories 300 • Calories from Fat 120 • Total Fat 13 g •
Saturated Fat 3 g • Cholesterol 50 mg • Sodium 380 mg • Dietary Fiber 1 g
Dietary Exchanges: 1¹/₂ Starch, 1 Fruit, 2¹/₂ Fat OR 2¹/₂ Carbohydrate, 2¹/₂ Fat

---

Overnight Coffee Cake Swirl

Prep Time: 20 minutes
(Ready in 8 hours 55 minutes)

Coffee Cake
1 cup all-purpose flour
¼ cup sugar
¼ cup firmly packed brown
  sugar
1 teaspoon baking powder
½ teaspoon baking soda
¼ teaspoon salt
½ cup buttermilk*

⅓ cup shortening
1 egg

Topping
¼ cup firmly packed brown
  sugar
¼ cup chopped nuts
¼ teaspoon nutmeg

1. Grease and flour 9-inch round or 8-inch square pan. In small bowl, combine all coffee cake ingredients; blend at low speed until moistened. Beat 2 minutes at medium speed. Pour batter into greased and floured pan.
2. In small bowl, combine all topping ingredients; blend well. Sprinkle over batter. Cover; refrigerate at least 8 hours or overnight.
3. Heat oven to 350°F. Uncover coffee cake; bake 25 to 35 minutes or until toothpick inserted in center comes out clean. Serve warm.

Yield: 8 servings
High Altitude (Above 3,500 Feet): No change.

Tip: *To substitute for buttermilk, use 1½ teaspoons vinegar or lemon juice plus milk to make ½ cup.

Nutrition Information Per Serving
Serving Size: ⅛ of Recipe. Calories 250 • Calories from Fat 110 • Total Fat 12 g •
Saturated Fat 3 g • Cholesterol 25 mg • Sodium 240 mg • Dietary Fiber 1 g
Dietary Exchanges: 1 Starch, 1 Fruit, 2½ Fat OR 2 Carbohydrate, 2½ Fat

Make-Ahead Tip

Here's a great recipe when you want a special breakfast but anticipate a rushed morning. Mix up the coffee cake batter and refrigerate it in the pan overnight, then simply pop it in the oven to bake in the morning.

Apple Streusel Coffee Cake

Prep Time: 20 minutes
(Ready in 1 hour 5 minutes)

Recipe Fact

Leaving the peel on the apples serves three purposes in this delicious coffee cake: it streamlines preparation, adds a touch of color and boosts the fiber content of the recipe.

Kitchen Tip

To prevent the apple slices from discoloring, slice them just before they're needed.

Make It Special

Top the cooled cake with a glaze made of powdered sugar and apple brandy (or another fruit-flavored brandy) or milk. Drizzle the glaze over the cake in a spiral or crosshatch design.

Coffee Cake
1 cup all-purpose flour
1 teaspoon baking powder
$\frac{1}{4}$ teaspoon baking soda
$\frac{1}{8}$ teaspoon salt
$\frac{1}{4}$ cup margarine or butter, softened
$\frac{1}{2}$ cup sugar
$\frac{1}{4}$ cup refrigerated or frozen fat-free egg product, thawed, or 1 egg
1 teaspoon vanilla
3 tablespoons nonfat plain yogurt
2 cups thinly sliced, unpeeled apples

Topping
$\frac{1}{4}$ cup all-purpose flour
2 tablespoons brown sugar
$\frac{1}{2}$ teaspoon cinnamon
2 tablespoons margarine or butter

1. Heat oven to 350°F. Spray 9-inch round or 8-inch square pan with nonstick cooking spray. In small bowl, combine 1 cup flour, baking powder, baking soda and salt; mix well. Set aside.

2. In large bowl, combine $\frac{1}{4}$ cup margarine and sugar; beat until light and fluffy. Add egg product and vanilla; blend well. Alternately add flour mixture and yogurt to margarine mixture, beating well after each addition. Spread batter in sprayed pan. Arrange apple slices over batter.

3. In small bowl, combine all topping ingredients except margarine. With pastry blender or fork, cut in 2 tablespoons margarine until crumbly. Sprinkle topping evenly over apples.

4. Bake at 350°F. for 30 to 35 minutes or until toothpick inserted in center comes out clean. Cool 10 minutes. If desired, remove from pan.

Yield: 8 servings
High Altitude (Above 3,500 Feet): No change.

Apple Streusel Coffee Cake

Blueberry-Poppy Seed Brunch Cake

Recipe Fact

There's a reason your guests will ooh and ahh over this cake: It's a real winner. Linda Rahman of Petaluma, California, won the $40,000 grand prize with this recipe at the 1990 Pillsbury Bake-Off® Contest. Poppy seed adds a subtle crunch and a nice flavor nuance to a sour cream coffee cake.

Prep Time: 30 minutes
(Ready in 1 hour 35 minutes)

Cake
$^2/_3$ cup sugar
$^1/_2$ cup margarine or butter, softened
2 teaspoons grated lemon peel
1 egg
$1^1/_2$ cups all-purpose flour
2 tablespoons poppy seed
$^1/_2$ teaspoon baking soda
$^1/_4$ teaspoon salt
$^1/_2$ cup sour cream

Filling
2 cups fresh or frozen blueberries, thawed, drained on paper towels
$^1/_3$ cup sugar
2 teaspoons all-purpose flour
$^1/_4$ teaspoon nutmeg

Glaze
$^1/_3$ cup powdered sugar
1 to 2 teaspoons milk

1. Heat oven to 350°F. Grease and flour bottom and sides of 9- or 10-inch springform pan. In large bowl, combine $^2/_3$ cup sugar and margarine; beat until light and fluffy. Add lemon peel and egg; beat 2 minutes at medium speed.
2. In medium bowl, combine $1^1/_2$ cups flour, poppy seed, baking soda and salt; mix well. Add to margarine mixture alternately with sour cream, beating well after each addition. Spread batter over bottom and 1 inch up sides of greased and floured pan, making sure batter on sides is $^1/_4$ inch thick.
3. In medium bowl, combine all filling ingredients; mix well. Spoon over batter.
4. Bake at 350°F. for 45 to 55 minutes or until crust is golden brown. Cool 10 minutes; remove sides of pan.
5. In small bowl, blend powdered sugar and enough milk for desired drizzling consistency. Drizzle over warm cake. Serve warm or cool.

Yield: 8 servings
High Altitude (Above 3,500 Feet): Increase flour in cake to $1^3/_4$ cups. Bake as directed above.

Blueberry-Poppy Seed Brunch Cake

Blueberry Muffin Cake

Prep Time: 25 minutes
(Ready in 1 hour 20 minutes)

Topping
¼ cup all-purpose flour
¼ cup sugar
½ teaspoon cinnamon
3 tablespoons margarine or butter

Cake
2 tablespoons fine, dry bread crumbs
2 cups all-purpose flour
1 cup sugar
3 teaspoons baking powder
½ teaspoon baking soda
½ teaspoon salt
½ teaspoon cinnamon
1 cup fresh or frozen blueberries, thawed, drained
2 eggs
⅓ cup orange-flavored liqueur or orange juice
¼ cup margarine or butter, melted, cooled
1 (8-oz.) container sour cream
1 teaspoon grated orange peel

1. In small bowl, combine all topping ingredients except margarine; mix well. With pastry blender or fork, cut in 3 tablespoons margarine until mixture resembles coarse crumbs. Set aside.

2. Heat oven to 375°F. Grease 10-inch springform pan or 9-inch square pan. Sprinkle with bread crumbs. In large bowl, combine 2 cups flour, 1 cup sugar, baking powder, baking soda, salt and ½ teaspoon cinnamon; mix well. Stir in blueberries.

3. Beat eggs in medium bowl. Stir in orange liqueur, ¼ cup margarine, sour cream and orange peel. Add to blueberry mixture; stir just until dry ingredients are moistened. Spoon batter into greased pan. Sprinkle with topping.

4. Bake at 375°F. for 35 to 45 minutes or until toothpick inserted in center comes out clean. Cool 10 minutes; remove sides of pan. Serve warm or cool.

Yield: 12 servings
High Altitude (Above 3,500 Feet): Decrease baking powder to 2 teaspoons.
Bake as directed above.

Nutrition Information Per Serving

Serving Size: $\frac{1}{12}$ of Recipe. Calories 320 • Calories from Fat 110 • Total Fat 12 g •
Saturated Fat 4 g • Cholesterol 45 mg • Sodium 370 mg • Dietary Fiber 1 g
Dietary Exchanges: 1½ Starch, 1½ Fruit, 2½ Fat OR 3 Carbohydrate, 2½ Fat

Blueberry Muffin Cake

Peach 'n Blueberry Coffee Cake

Prep Time: 25 minutes
(Ready in 1 hour 40 minutes)

Coffee Cake
2 cups all-purpose flour
1 cup sugar
2 teaspoons baking powder
1 teaspoon salt
1½ teaspoons grated orange
  peel
½ cup margarine or butter,
  softened
1 cup milk
1 teaspoon vanilla

2 eggs, slightly beaten
1 cup fresh or frozen sliced
  peaches, thawed
1 cup fresh or frozen
  blueberries, thawed

Glaze
1 cup powdered sugar
¼ teaspoon almond extract
3 to 5 teaspoons milk

1. Heat oven to 350°F. Grease 13 × 9-inch pan. In large bowl, combine flour, sugar, baking powder, salt and orange peel; mix well. With pastry blender or fork, cut in margarine until crumbly.

2. Add milk, vanilla and eggs; stir until dry ingredients are moistened. Pour ¾ of batter (2¼ cups) into greased pan. Top with peaches and blueberries. Spoon remaining batter over fruit.

3. Bake at 350°F. for 35 to 45 minutes or until edges are golden brown. Cool 30 minutes.

4. In small bowl, blend all glaze ingredients, adding enough milk for desired drizzling consistency. Drizzle over coffee cake.

Yield: 12 servings
High Altitude (Above 3,500 Feet): Bake at 375°F. for 30 to 35 minutes.

Nutrition Information Per Serving
Serving Size: ¹⁄₁₂ of Recipe. Calories 290 • Calories from Fat 80 • Total Fat 9 g • Saturated Fat 2 g • Cholesterol 35 mg • Sodium 370 mg • Dietary Fiber 1 g
Dietary Exchanges: 2 Starch, 1 Fruit, 1½ Fat OR 3 Carbohydrate, 1½ Fat

About Frozen Fruit

Frozen blueberries and peaches are convenient when you want to make this coffee cake and the fresh fruit is out of season. It doesn't matter that the freezing makes the fruit's texture softer; the fruit becomes soft when cooked, anyway. As a refreshing low-fat snack, partially thaw the fruit and munch delightful little bites of guilt-free frozen pops!

Ingredient Substitution

Almond extract's nutty essence is especially suited to fruit recipes and angel food cakes. If you're not a fan of its strong flavor, substitute vanilla in the glaze.

Make It Special

Welcome a new family to the neighborhood with a Peach 'n Blueberry Coffee Cake accompanied by a small jar of peach preserves and a pint of fresh berries.

Peach 'n Blueberry Coffee Cake

Cranberry-Pear Coffee Cake

Prep Time: 20 minutes
(Ready in 50 minutes)

Ingredient Substitution

Crushed vanilla wafer cookies can be used instead of the graham cracker crumbs.

Make It Special

Scoop vanilla ice cream or frozen yogurt on each piece of cake; drizzle with Poire William (pear liqueur) or your preferred liqueur.

Topping
1 cup chopped peeled pears
1 teaspoon lemon juice
1/2 cup sweetened dried cranberries
1/4 cup graham cracker crumbs
2 tablespoons brown sugar
1 tablespoon all-purpose flour
1/4 teaspoon allspice
1/8 teaspoon ginger

Cake
1/3 cup sugar
1/4 cup margarine or butter
2 egg whites
1/4 teaspoon lemon extract or
    1 teaspoon grated lemon peel
3/4 cup all-purpose flour
1/4 cup graham cracker crumbs
1 teaspoon baking soda
1/4 teaspoon salt
1/4 teaspoon allspice
1/8 teaspoon ginger
1/4 cup skim milk

1. Heat oven to 350° F. Spray 9 or 8-inch square pan with nonstick cooking spray. In medium bowl, combine pears and lemon juice; toss gently to coat. Add all remaining topping ingredients; mix lightly. Set aside.

2. In large bowl, combine sugar and margarine; beat at medium speed until well blended. Add egg whites and lemon extract; blend well. Add all remaining cake ingredients; mix well. Pour batter into sprayed pan. Spoon topping evenly over batter.

3. Bake at 350° F. for 25 to 30 minutes or until top is golden brown and toothpick inserted in center comes out clean. Serve warm or cool.

Yield: 12 servings

High Altitude (Above 3,500 Feet): Increase flour in cake to 3/4 cup plus 2 tablespoons. **Bake as directed above.**

Nutrition Information Per Serving
Serving Size: 1/12 of Recipe. Calories 140 • Calories from Fat 35 • Total Fat 4 g • Saturated Fat 1 g • Cholesterol 0 mg • Sodium 230 mg • Dietary Fiber 1 g
Dietary Exchanges: 1 Starch, 1/2 Fruit, 1/2 Fat OR 1 1/2 Carbohydrate, 1/2 Fat

Lemony Raspberry Coffee Cake

Prep Time: 25 minutes
(Ready in 1 hour 10 minutes)

⅓ cup sugar
¼ cup refrigerated or frozen fat-free egg product, thawed, or 1 egg
¼ cup oil
2 tablespoons grated lemon peel
1 tablespoon lemon juice

1 (8-oz.) container low-fat lemon yogurt
1¾ cups all-purpose flour
2 teaspoons baking powder
½ teaspoon baking soda
¼ teaspoon salt
⅔ cup low-sugar red raspberry preserves

1. Heat oven to 350°F. In medium bowl, combine sugar, egg product and oil; beat well. Stir in lemon peel, lemon juice and yogurt.

2. Add flour, baking powder, baking soda and salt; stir just until dry ingredients are moistened. Spread half of batter in ungreased 9-inch round cake pan.

3. Reserve ⅓ cup preserves for top of cake. Carefully spread remaining ⅓ cup preserves over batter to within ¼ inch of edge of pan. Spoon remaining batter over top, spreading to cover preserves completely.

4. Bake at 350°F. for 25 to 35 minutes or until toothpick inserted in center comes out clean. Spread reserved ⅓ cup preserves over top of cake. Cool 10 minutes. Serve warm.

Yield: 8 servings
High Altitude (Above 3,500 Feet): No change.

Nutrition Information Per Serving

Serving Size: ⅛ of Recipe. Calories 260 • Calories from Fat 60 • Total Fat 7 g •
Saturated Fat 1 g • Cholesterol 0 mg • Sodium 380 mg • Dietary Fiber 1 g
Dietary Exchanges: 2 Starch, 1 Fruit, 1 Fat OR 3 Carbohydrate, 1 Fat

About Low-Sugar Preserves

Don't be fooled into thinking that "low-sugar" or "all-fruit" preserves are healthy while traditional with-sugar preserves are not. Fruit contains so much natural sugar that, by the time all-fruit preserves are processed, the nutritional profile of no-sugar and regular preserves are virtually identical. The chief advantage in low-sugar or all-fruit varieties is that the fruit flavor tends to be more intense. Sample to know for sure.

Ingredient Substitution

If raspberry preserves are not available, try strawberry, blackberry or apricot preserves instead.

About Lemon Curd

Lemon curd, a British specialty, is an intensely rich, intensely sweet blend of lemon, egg yolk and butter that's often used as a tart filling or dessert topping. Because it's so rich, it's best used in small amounts.

Make It Special

If you wish, toast the coconut before stirring it into the streusel mixture. Spread the flakes onto a baking sheet and bake at 350°F. for 10 minutes or until the flakes begin to turn golden brown.

Ingredient Substitution

Lemon pie filling can be substituted for the lemon curd.

Menu Suggestion

Serve the cake with espresso and fresh raspberries.

Lemon Surprise Coffee Cake

Prep Time: 30 minutes
(Ready in 2 hours 40 minutes)

Streusel
½ cup all-purpose flour
⅓ cup sugar
3 tablespoons butter
½ cup coconut

Coffee Cake
2¼ cups all-purpose flour
1 cup sugar
½ teaspoon baking powder
½ teaspoon baking soda
½ teaspoon salt

¾ cup butter, softened
⅔ cup vanilla yogurt
2 teaspoons grated lemon peel
1 tablespoon lemon juice
1 egg
1 egg yolk
½ cup purchased lemon curd

Glaze
½ cup powdered sugar
1 teaspoon lemon juice
1 teaspoon water

1. Heat oven to 350°F. Grease and flour 10 or 9-inch springform pan. In medium bowl, combine ½ cup flour and ⅓ cup sugar; mix well. With pastry blender or fork, cut in 3 tablespoons butter until mixture resembles coarse crumbs. Stir in coconut.

2. In large bowl, combine 2¼ cups flour, 1 cup sugar, baking powder, baking soda and salt; mix well. Add ¾ cup butter, yogurt, lemon peel, 1 tablespoon lemon juice, egg and yolk; stir with spoon until well blended.

3. Spread 2 cups of the batter in greased and floured pan. Sprinkle with ¾ cup of the streusel. Drop lemon curd by ½ teaspoonfuls over streusel to within ½ inch of edge. Spoon remaining batter over lemon curd. Sprinkle with remaining streusel.

4. Bake at 350°F. for 50 to 60 minutes or until toothpick inserted in center comes out clean. Cool 10 minutes; remove sides of pan.

5. In small bowl, combine all glaze ingredients; blend until smooth. Drizzle over warm coffee cake. Cool 1 hour. Serve warm.

Yield: 12 servings
High Altitude (Above 3,500 Feet): No change.

Nutrition Information Per Serving

Serving Size: $\frac{1}{12}$ of Recipe. Calories 420 • Calories from Fat 150 • Total Fat 17 g •
Saturated Fat 10 g • Cholesterol 75 mg • Sodium 340 mg • Dietary Fiber 1 g
Dietary Exchanges: 2 Starch, 2 Fruit, 3 Fat OR 4 Carbohydrate, 3 Fat

Lemon Surprise Coffee Cake

Golden Pineapple-Carrot Coffee Cake

Prep Time: 25 minutes
(Ready in 1 hour 10 minutes)

Cake
⅓ cup sugar
¼ cup refrigerated or frozen
   fat-free egg product,
   thawed, or 1 egg
3 tablespoons oil
1 cup shredded carrots
1 (8-oz.) can crushed pineapple
   in unsweetened juice,
   undrained
⅓ cup orange juice
1½ cups all-purpose flour
1½ teaspoons baking soda
1 teaspoon cinnamon
¼ teaspoon salt

Topping
⅓ cup sugar
⅓ cup finely chopped walnuts
¾ teaspoon cinnamon

1. Heat oven to 350°F. Spray 9-inch round cake pan with nonstick cooking spray.
2. In medium bowl, combine ⅓ cup sugar, egg product and oil; mix well. Add carrots, pineapple and orange juice; blend well.
3. In small bowl, combine flour, baking soda, 1 teaspoon cinnamon and salt; mix well. Add to carrot-pineapple mixture; stir just until dry ingredients are moistened. Spread batter evenly in sprayed pan.
4. In another small bowl, combine all topping ingredients; mix well. Sprinkle over batter.
5. Bake at 350°F. for 25 to 35 minutes or until toothpick inserted in center comes out clean. Cool 10 minutes. Serve warm.

Yield: 8 servings
High Altitude (Above 3,500 Feet): No change.

Nutrition Information Per Serving
Serving Size: ⅛ of Recipe. Calories 260 • Calories from Fat 70 • Total Fat 8 g •
Saturated Fat 1 g • Cholesterol 0 mg • Sodium 320 mg • Dietary Fiber 2 g
Dietary Exchanges: 2 Starch, 1 Fruit, 1 Fat OR 3 Carbohydrate, 1 Fat

Orange-Pineapple Muffin Cake

Prep Time: 20 minutes
(Ready in 50 minutes)

Cake

1½ cups all-purpose flour
1 cup whole wheat flour
⅓ cup firmly packed brown
    sugar
3 teaspoons baking powder
½ teaspoon baking soda
¼ teaspoon salt
1 (8.25-oz.) can crushed
    pineapple, drained

½ cup orange juice
⅓ cup margarine, melted
½ to 1 teaspoon grated orange
    peel
1 egg, slightly beaten

Glaze

½ cup powdered sugar
½ teaspoon grated orange peel
1 to 2 tablespoons orange juice

• editor's favorite   • gift idea

Recipe Fact

Whole wheat flour adds texture and wholesomeness to this muffinlike cake.

Make It Special

Dip walnut or pecan halves into the glaze and use one on each serving as a decoration.

1. Heat oven to 400°F. Grease bottom only of 9-inch springform pan or 9-inch round cake pan. In large bowl, combine all-purpose flour, whole wheat flour, brown sugar, baking powder, baking soda and salt; mix well.
2. In medium bowl, combine all remaining cake ingredients; blend well. Add to flour mixture all at once; stir just until dry ingredients are moistened. Spoon and spread batter evenly in greased pan.
3. Bake at 400°F. for 22 to 27 minutes or until top is light golden brown and toothpick inserted in center comes out clean. Cool 1 minute; remove from pan.
4. In small bowl, combine all glaze ingredients, adding enough orange juice for desired drizzling consistency. Drizzle over warm cake. If desired, garnish with orange slices and mint leaves. Serve warm.

Yield: 12 servings
High Altitude (Above 3,500 Feet): Decrease baking powder to 2 teaspoons.
Bake as directed above.

Nutrition Information Per Serving

Serving Size: 1/12 of Recipe. Calories 210 • Calories from Fat 50 • Total Fat 6 g •
Saturated Fat 1 g • Cholesterol 20 mg • Sodium 290 mg • Dietary Fiber 2 g
Dietary Exchanges: 1 Starch, 1½ Fruit, 1 Fat OR 2½ Carbohydrate, 1 Fat

Raspberry Breakfast Cake

Prep Time: 25 minutes
(Ready in 1 hour 40 minutes)

Recipe Fact

It's best to serve this rich, moist cake slightly warm and freshly frosted.

Ingredient Substitution

The cake is also delicious made with fresh or frozen blueberries.

Recipe Variation

Instead of flavoring the frosting with lemon juice, stir in an equal amount of orange liqueur.

Cake
¾ cup sugar
½ cup margarine or butter, softened
3 eggs
⅓ cup (1 small) mashed ripe banana
¼ cup milk
¼ cup sour cream
1 teaspoon almond extract
2 cups all-purpose flour

1½ teaspoons baking powder
1½ cups fresh or frozen raspberries, thawed, drained

Frosting
1 cup powdered sugar
¼ cup margarine or butter, softened
1 to 2 teaspoons lemon juice

1. Heat oven to 350°F. Grease and flour a 9-inch square pan. In a large bowl, combine sugar, ½ cup margarine, eggs and banana; beat until light and fluffy. Add milk, sour cream and almond extract; beat until well blended.
2. Add flour and baking powder; stir just until dry ingredients are moistened. Pour half of batter into greased and floured pan. Sprinkle raspberries over batter. Pour remaining batter over raspberries.
3. Bake at 350°F. for 50 to 55 minutes or until top is deep golden brown. Cool 20 minutes.
4. Meanwhile, in small bowl, combine powdered sugar and ¼ cup margarine; beat until well blended. Add enough lemon juice for desired spreading consistency. Spread over warm cake. Serve warm.

Yield: 9 servings
High Altitude (Above 3,500 Feet): No change.

Nutrition Information Per Serving
Serving Size: ⅑ of Recipe. Calories 420 • Calories from Fat 170 • Total Fat 19 g •
Saturated Fat 4 g • Cholesterol 75 mg • Sodium 290 mg • Dietary Fiber 2 g
Dietary Exchanges: 2 Starch, 1½ Fruit, 3½ Fat OR 3½ Carbohydrate, 3½ Fat

Raspberry Breakfast Cake

Raspberry Cream Cheese Coffee Cake

Prep Time: 25 minutes
(Ready in 1 hour 35 minutes)

Ingredient Substitution

Apricot preserves go equally well with the cream cheese filling and sliced almonds.

Storage Tip

Always remember to store baked goods that have cheese fillings in the refrigerator.

2¼ cups all-purpose flour
¾ cup sugar
¾ cup margarine or butter
½ teaspoon baking powder
½ teaspoon baking soda
¼ teaspoon salt
¾ cup sour cream
1 teaspoon almond extract

1 egg
1 (8-oz.) pkg. cream cheese, softened
¼ cup sugar
1 egg
½ cup raspberry preserves
½ cup sliced almonds

1. Heat oven to 350°F. Grease and flour bottom and sides of 9 or 10-inch springform pan. In large bowl, combine flour and ¾ cup sugar; mix well. With pastry blender or fork, cut in margarine until mixture resembles coarse crumbs. Reserve 1 cup of crumb mixture.

2. To remaining crumb mixture, add baking powder, baking soda, salt, sour cream, almond extract and 1 egg; blend well. Spread batter over bottom and 2 inches up sides (about ¼ inch thick) of greased and floured pan.

3. In small bowl, combine cream cheese, ¼ cup sugar and 1 egg; blend well. Pour into batter-lined pan. Carefully spoon preserves evenly over cream cheese mixture.

4. In small bowl, combine reserved crumb mixture and sliced almonds. Sprinkle over preserves.

5. Bake at 350°F. for 45 to 55 minutes or until cream cheese filling is set and crust is deep golden brown. Cool 15 minutes; remove sides of pan. Store in refrigerator.

Yield: 16 servings
High Altitude (Above 3,500 Feet): No change.

Nutrition Information Per Serving

Serving Size: ¹⁄₁₆ of Recipe. Calories 320 • Calories from Fat 160 • Total Fat 18 g • Saturated Fat 7 g • Cholesterol 45 mg • Sodium 250 mg • Dietary Fiber 1 g
Dietary Exchanges: 1½ Starch, 1 Fruit, 3½ Fat OR 2½ Carbohydrate, 3½ Fat

Whole Wheat Rhubarb Coffee Cake

Prep Time: 25 minutes
(Ready in 1 hour 10 minutes)

Coffee Cake
½ cup firmly packed brown
  sugar
¼ cup refrigerated or frozen
  fat-free egg product,
  thawed, or 1 egg
¼ cup oil
⅔ cup skim milk
1 cup whole wheat flour
¾ cup all-purpose flour
3 teaspoons baking powder

½ teaspoon baking soda
¼ teaspoon salt
2 cups fresh or frozen sliced
  rhubarb

Glaze
1 tablespoon margarine or
  butter, softened
1 cup powdered sugar
1 tablespoon skim milk
½ teaspoon vanilla

1. Heat oven to 350°F. Spray 9-inch square pan with non-stick cooking spray. In medium bowl, combine brown sugar and egg product; beat until light. Slowly add oil, beating until well blended. Stir in ⅔ cup milk.

2. Add whole wheat flour, all-purpose flour, baking powder, baking soda and salt; stir just until dry ingredients are moistened. Fold in rhubarb. Spoon and spread batter evenly in sprayed pan.

3. Bake at 350°F. for 25 to 35 minutes or until cake springs back when touched lightly in center.

4. In small bowl, combine all glaze ingredients; beat until smooth. Spread glaze evenly over top of hot cake. Cool 10 minutes. Serve warm.

Yield: 9 servings
High Altitude (Above 3,500 Feet): Increase all-purpose flour to 1 cup.
Bake as directed above.

Make It Special
Sprinkle the glaze with minced toasted walnuts, roasted sunflower seeds or sliced toasted almonds.

Ingredient Substitutions
Substitute frozen rhubarb for fresh; bake at 350°F. for 35 to 45 minutes.

This cake will also taste good made with raspberries instead of rhubarb.

Menu Suggestion
Serve the cake with vanilla frozen yogurt and coffee or tea following a spring meal of grilled or broiled salmon, new potatoes, steamed fresh peas and baby lettuces tossed with balsamic vinaigrette.

Nutrition Information Per Serving
Serving Size: ⅑ of Recipe. Calories 270 • Calories from Fat 70 • Total Fat 8 g •
Saturated Fat 1 g • Cholesterol 0 mg • Sodium 330 mg • Dietary Fiber 2 g
Dietary Exchanges: 1½ Starch, 1½ Fruit, 1½ Fat OR 3 Carbohydrate, 1½ Fat

Pumpkin-Date Coffee Cake

Prep Time: 25 minutes
(Ready in 1 hour 40 minutes)

Topping
¼ cup all-purpose flour
¼ cup sugar
½ teaspoon cinnamon
3 tablespoons margarine or
butter

Coffee Cake
2 cups all-purpose flour
1 cup sugar
3 teaspoons baking powder
1 teaspoon pumpkin pie spice
½ teaspoon baking soda
½ teaspoon salt

2 eggs
1 cup canned pumpkin
⅓ cup orange juice
¼ cup margarine or butter,
melted, cooled
1 teaspoon grated orange peel
1 cup chopped nuts
½ cup chopped dates

Glaze
½ cup powdered sugar
1 teaspoon grated orange peel
1 to 2 tablespoons orange juice

1. In small bowl, combine all topping ingredients except margarine; mix well. With pastry blender or fork, cut in 3 tablespoons margarine until mixture resembles coarse crumbs. Set aside.

2. Heat oven to 375°F. Grease 10-inch tube pan. In large bowl, combine 2 cups flour, 1 cup sugar, baking powder, pumpkin pie spice, baking soda and salt; mix well.

3. Beat eggs in small bowl. Stir in pumpkin, ⅓ cup orange juice, ¼ cup margarine and 1 teaspoon orange peel. Add to flour mixture; stir just until dry ingredients are moistened. Stir in nuts and dates. Spoon and spread batter in greased pan. Sprinkle with crumb topping.

4. Bake at 375°F. for 40 to 45 minutes or until toothpick inserted in center comes out clean. Cool 30 minutes; remove from pan.

5. In small bowl, blend all glaze ingredients, adding enough orange juice for desired drizzling consistency. Drizzle over warm coffee cake. Serve warm or cool.

Yield: 12 servings
High Altitude (Above 3,500 Feet): No change.

Nutrition Information Per Serving

Serving Size: $\frac{1}{12}$ of Recipe. Calories 360 • Calories from Fat 130 • Total Fat 14 g • Saturated Fat 2 g • Cholesterol 35 mg • Sodium 350 mg • Dietary Fiber 2 g
Dietary Exchanges: 1½ Starch, 2 Fruit, 2½ Fat OR 3½ Carbohydrate, 2½ Fat

Bran Muffin Cake

Prep Time: 15 minutes
(Ready in 1 hour 10 minutes)

Recipe Fact

This popular muffin flavor is quick to serve for breakfast when it's baked as a coffee cake and cut into wedges.

Ingredient Substitution

Substitute chopped dried apricots or dried cranberries for the golden raisins.

Make It Special

For a new take on the day, start out with a picnic breakfast! Pack up a Bran Muffin Cake, hard-cooked eggs, fresh fruit or juice and a thermos of coffee and head for the beach or nearby park.

Cake

- 1½ cups shreds of whole bran cereal
- 1¼ cups skim milk
- ¾ cup golden raisins
- ½ cup sugar
- 3 tablespoons margarine or butter
- 2 egg whites
- 1 egg
- 2 cups all-purpose flour
- 2 teaspoons baking powder
- ½ teaspoon baking soda
- ½ teaspoon salt
- ½ teaspoon cinnamon
- ½ teaspoon nutmeg

Topping

- 1 tablespoon sugar
- ½ teaspoon cinnamon

1. Heat oven to 375°F. Lightly grease and flour 9-inch round cake pan. In medium bowl, combine cereal, milk and raisins; mix well. Set aside.

2. In large bowl, combine ½ cup sugar and margarine; beat at medium speed until light and fluffy. Add egg whites and egg; mix until smooth. Add all remaining cake ingredients; stir just until combined. Stir in cereal mixture just until blended. Spoon and spread batter evenly in greased and floured pan.

3. In small bowl, combine topping ingredients; mix well. Sprinkle over batter.

4. Bake at 375°F. for 35 to 45 minutes or until toothpick inserted in center comes out clean. Cool 10 minutes. Serve warm.

Yield: 8 servings
High Altitude (Above 3,500 Feet): No change.

Nutrition Information Per Serving

Serving Size: ⅛ of Recipe. Calories 350 • Calories from Fat 50 • Total Fat 6 g • Saturated Fat 1 g • Cholesterol 25 mg • Sodium 460 mg • Dietary Fiber 7 g
Dietary Exchanges: 3 Starch, 1 Fruit, 1 Fat OR 4 Carbohydrate, 1 Fat

Banana-Raisin Bran Coffee Cake

Prep Time: 20 minutes
(Ready in 1 hour 5 minutes)

fiber source

Coffee Cake
½ cup milk
1 egg
3 tablespoons oil
1½ cups bran flakes cereal
½ cup (1 medium) mashed ripe banana
1½ cups all-purpose flour
¼ cup firmly packed brown sugar
2 teaspoons baking powder
½ teaspoon cinnamon
¼ teaspoon baking soda
¼ teaspoon salt
½ cup raisins, if desired

Topping
⅔ cup bran flakes cereal, finely crushed
2 tablespoons brown sugar
1 tablespoon margarine or butter, melted
⅛ teaspoon cinnamon

Recipe Fact
The breakfast combo of bananas and bran flakes also creates a great-tasting coffee cake.

Recipe Variation
For a cake with more crunch, add ½ cup roasted sunflower seeds or nuts to the batter.

1. Heat oven to 350°F. Spray 9-inch round cake pan with nonstick cooking spray. In medium bowl, combine milk, egg product and oil; beat until well blended. Stir in 1½ cups cereal and banana until well mixed. Set aside.

2. In large bowl, combine flour, ¼ cup brown sugar, baking powder, cinnamon, baking soda and salt; mix well. Stir in raisins. Add banana mixture; stir just until dry ingredients are moistened. Spoon and spread batter evenly in sprayed pan.

3. In small bowl, combine all topping ingredients; mix well. Sprinkle over batter.

4. Bake at 350°F. for 25 to 35 minutes or until cake springs back when touched lightly in center. Cool 10 minutes. Serve warm.

Yield: 8 servings
High Altitude (Above 3,500 Feet): No change.

Nutrition Information Per Serving
Serving Size: ⅛ of Recipe. Calories 280 • Calories from Fat 70 • Total Fat 8 g • Saturated Fat 1 g • Cholesterol 30 mg • Sodium 340 mg • Dietary Fiber 3 g
Dietary Exchanges: 2 Starch, 1 Fruit, 1½ Fat OR 3 Carbohydrate, 1½ Fat

Apple Yogurt Kuchen

Prep Time: 25 minutes
(Ready in 1 hour 20 minutes)

About Cooking Apples

If you want the apples to retain their shape and remain flavorful during baking, choose Rome Beauty, Winesap, Granny Smith or Jonathan. If you prefer softer cooked apples, try McIntosh or Cortland.

Kitchen Tip

A springform pan has two pieces: a base and a cylindrical side piece. The side piece has a spring mechanism—a type of latch—that holds the sides tightly around the base while the cake is cooking. After the cake has cooled, release the latch to open the sides for easy removal. The base of the pan can remain in place during serving.

Kuchen

½ cup margarine or butter, softened
¼ cup sugar
1 teaspoon vanilla
1 egg
1 cup all-purpose flour
½ teaspoon baking powder
¼ teaspoon salt

Filling

½ cup vanilla yogurt
1 egg
1½ cups thinly sliced, peeled apples
3 tablespoons sugar
1 teaspoon cinnamon

1. Heat oven to 350°F. Grease 9-inch springform pan. In large bowl, combine margarine and ¼ cup sugar; beat until light and fluffy. Add vanilla and 1 egg; beat well. Stir in flour, baking powder and salt; mix well. Spread dough over bottom and 1 inch up sides of pan.

2. In small bowl, combine yogurt and 1 egg; spread over dough. Arrange apple slices over filling; sprinkle with 3 tablespoons sugar and cinnamon.

3. Bake at 350°F. for 35 to 45 minutes or until edges are golden brown. Cool 10 minutes; remove sides of pan. Serve warm or cool. Store in refrigerator.

Yield: 8 servings
High Altitude (Above 3,500 Feet): No change.

Nutrition Information Per Serving

Serving Size: ⅛ of Recipe. Calories 250 • Calories from Fat 120 • Total Fat 13 g • Saturated Fat 3 g • Cholesterol 55 mg • Sodium 260 mg • Dietary Fiber 1 g Dietary Exchanges: 1½ Starch, ½ Fruit, 2½ Fat OR 2 Carbohydrate, 2½ Fat

Pear-Cardamom Kuchen

Prep Time: 25 minutes
(Ready in 1 hour 15 minutes)

Kuchen

½ cup margarine or butter,
 softened
¼ cup sugar
1 teaspoon vanilla
1 egg
1 cup all-purpose flour
1 teaspoon cardamom
½ teaspoon baking powder

¼ teaspoon salt
1 (29-oz.) can pear halves, well
 drained, sliced

Topping

3 tablespoons sugar
½ teaspoon cardamom
⅛ teaspoon cinnamon

1. Heat oven to 350°F. Grease 9-inch springform pan. In medium bowl, combine margarine and ¼ cup sugar; beat until light and fluffy. Add vanilla and egg; beat well.

2. In small bowl, combine flour, 1 teaspoon cardamom, baking powder and salt; mix well. Gradually add to margarine mixture, mixing well. Spread batter over bottom and 1 inch up sides of greased pan. Arrange sliced pears over batter.

3. In small bowl, combine all topping ingredients; mix well. Sprinkle over pears.

4. Bake at 350°F. for 35 to 40 minutes or until edges are golden brown. Cool 10 minutes; remove sides of pan. Serve warm or cool.

Yield: 8 servings
High Altitude (Above 3,500 Feet): No change.

Nutrition Information Per Serving

Serving Size: ⅛ of Recipe. Calories 240 • Calories from Fat 110 • Total Fat 12 g • Saturated Fat 2 g • Cholesterol 25 mg • Sodium 240 mg • Dietary Fiber 2 g Dietary Exchanges: 1 Starch, 1 Fruit, 2 Fat OR 2 Carbohydrate, 2 Fat

Recipe Fact

This fragrant cake combines a simplified version of the yeast-raised German specialty kuchen with the Scandinavian flavor of cardamom.

Recipe Variation

Make the kuchen with drained canned apricot halves or peach slices instead of the pear halves.

Butters and Spreads

As a sweet ending to this book, the following toppings can help you gild the lily. All are made with butter or cream cheese plus flavorings. The key to success with any of them is to make sure the butter or cream cheese is thoroughly soft before you attempt to beat in the remaining ingredients.

Butters and Spreads

Previous page: Cranberry-Orange Butter, page 230; Chocolate-Honey Butter, page 229; Lemon-Spiced Cream Cheese Spread, page 234

Whipped Butter

Prep Time: 5 minutes

½ cup butter, softened   **2 tablespoons milk or cream**

In small bowl, combine butter and milk; beat at high speed until light and fluffy.

Yield: 1 cup

Nutrition Information Per Serving
Serving Size: 1 Tablespoon. Calories 50 • Calories from Fat 50 • Total Fat 6 g • Saturated Fat 4 g • Cholesterol 15 mg • Sodium 60 mg • Dietary Fiber 0 g Dietary Exchange: 1 Fat

Variations

Apricot Butter: Omit milk; gradually add ¼ cup apricot preserves, beating until light and fluffy.

Honey Butter: Omit milk; gradually add ¼ cup honey, beating until light and fluffy.

Maple Butter: Substitute maple-flavored syrup for milk.

Marmalade Butter: Omit milk; gradually add ¼ cup orange marmalade, beating until light and fluffy.

Orange Butter: Substitute orange juice for milk; add 1 tablespoon grated orange peel.

Raspberry Butter: Omit milk; gradually add ¼ cup seedless raspberry jam, beating until light and fluffy.

Make It Special

For a festive brunch, make several flavored whipped butters and offer them with a selection of muffins and breads.

Recipe Variation

For flavored whipped butter to enhance baked potatoes, steamed vegetables or savory breads and biscuits, beat 1 tablespoon minced fresh herbs into basic butter.

Amaretto Butter

Prep Time: 10 minutes

About Amaretto

Amaretto, an almond-flavored Italian liqueur, is nice as an after-dinner cordial, either solo or stirred into a cup of coffee.

Recipe Variation

Make the flavored butter with Frangelico (hazelnut liqueur) instead of amaretto.

½ cup butter, softened
¼ cup powdered sugar

3 tablespoons amaretto or
½ teaspoon almond extract
and 2 tablespoons water

In small bowl, beat butter until light and fluffy. Gradually beat in powdered sugar and amaretto.

Yield: 1 cup

Nutrition Information Per Serving

Serving Size: 1 Tablespoon. Calories 70 • Calories from Fat 50 • Total Fat 6 g • Saturated Fat 4 g • Cholesterol 15 mg • Sodium 60 mg • Dietary Fiber 0 g
Dietary Exchange: 1½ Fat

Brandy Butter

Prep Time: 10 minutes

Recipe Variation

Substitute a flavored brandy of choice for the plain brandy.

Menu Suggestion

Serve this butter with your favorite muffin or quick bread made with fruit or nuts. It goes well on pancakes, too!

½ cup butter, softened
2 tablespoons brown sugar

2 tablespoons brandy

In small bowl, beat butter until light and fluffy. Add brown sugar; beat well. Gradually add brandy, blending well.

Yield: About ¾ cup

Nutrition Information Per Serving

Serving Size: 1 Tablespoon. Calories 90 • Calories from Fat 70 • Total Fat 8 g • Saturated Fat 5 g • Cholesterol 20 mg • Sodium 80 mg • Dietary Fiber 0 g
Dietary Exchange: 2 Fat

Chocolate-Honey Butter

gift idea

Prep Time: 5 minutes

½ cup butter, softened
2 tablespoons honey

2 tablespoons chocolate-flavored syrup

In small bowl, combine all ingredients; beat at high speed until light and fluffy.

Yield: 1 cup

Nutrition Information Per Serving
Serving Size: 1 Tablespoon. Calories 70 • Calories from Fat 50 • Total Fat 6 g •
Saturated Fat 4 g • Cholesterol 15 mg • Sodium 60 mg • Dietary Fiber 0 g
Dietary Exchanges: ½ Fruit, 1 Fat OR ½ Carbohydrate, 1 Fat

Recipe Variation

Stir 2 tablespoons miniature chocolate chips or minced nuts into the butter.

Cinnamon-Honey Butter

Prep Time: 5 minutes

1 cup butter, softened
⅓ cup honey

2 teaspoons cinnamon

In medium bowl, combine all ingredients; beat until light and fluffy. DO NOT OVERMIX.

Yield: About 1½ cups

Nutrition Information Per Serving
Serving Size: 1 Tablespoon. Calories 90 • Calories from Fat 70 • Total Fat 8 g •
Saturated Fat 5 g • Cholesterol 20 mg • Sodium 80 mg • Dietary Fiber 0 g
Dietary Exchanges: ½ Fruit, 1½ Fat OR ½ Carbohydrate, 1½ Fat

Kitchen Tip

A wooden spoon works best for beating the butter. Not only would an electric mixer overbeat the mixture, but the butter would tend to clump up in the beater blades.

Menu Suggestion

Pair this spiced spread with cornbread, baking powder biscuits or fruited muffins.

Cranberry-Orange Butter

editor's favorite • gift idea

Prep Time: 10 minutes

Make It Special

While the mixture is still soft, pipe it into a serving dish for the center of the table, or pipe individual swirls or rosettes as garnishes for each plate. Restaurants often serve pats of butter on ice, but it's easier for guests to spread if you serve it at room temperature.

½ cup butter, softened
3 tablespoons whole berry
   cranberry sauce

1 teaspoon grated orange peel

In small bowl, beat butter until light and fluffy. Gradually beat in cranberry sauce and orange peel.

Yield: ¾ cup

Nutrition Information Per Serving
Serving Size: 1 Tablespoon. Calories 80 • Calories from Fat 70 • Total Fat 8 g • Saturated Fat 5 g • Cholesterol 20 mg • Sodium 80 mg • Dietary Fiber 0 g
Dietary Exchange: 1½ Fat

Cinnamon-Peach Butter

Prep Time: 5 minutes

Ingredient Substitution

If you wish, make this butter with another dried fruit instead of peaches. Dried apples, pears or apricots would all make interesting substitutions.

1 cup butter, softened
¼ cup finely chopped dried
   peaches

½ teaspoon cinnamon

In small bowl, combine all ingredients; beat until light and fluffy.

Yield: 1 cup

Nutrition Information Per Serving
Serving Size: 1 Tablespoon. Calories 120 • Calories from Fat 110 • Total Fat 12 g • Saturated Fat 7 g • Cholesterol 30 mg • Sodium 115 mg • Dietary Fiber 0 g
Dietary Exchange: 2½ Fat

Whipped Cream Cheese

Prep Time: 5 minutes

1 (8-oz.) pkg. cream cheese, softened

3 to 4 tablespoons milk

In small bowl, beat cream cheese until soft. Gradually beat in enough milk until light and fluffy.

Yield: 1½ cups

> ### Nutrition Information Per Serving
> Serving Size: 1 Tablespoon. Calories 30 • Calories from Fat 25 • Total Fat 3 g •
> Saturated Fat 2 g • Cholesterol 10 mg • Sodium 30 mg • Dietary Fiber 0 g
> Dietary Exchange: ½ Fat

Recipe Variation

For bagels or plain savory breads, blend the cream cheese with 2 tablespoons minced smoked salmon (lox), using more or less to taste.

Variations

Honey Cream Cheese: Omit milk; gradually add ¼ cup honey, beating until light and fluffy.

Maple Cream Cheese: Substitute maple-flavored syrup for milk.

Marmalade Cream Cheese: Omit milk; gradually add ¼ cup orange marmalade, beating until light and fluffy.

Orange Cream Cheese: Substitute orange juice for milk; add ½ teaspoon grated orange peel.

Strawberry Cream Cheese

Prep Time: 10 minutes

1 (8-oz.) pkg. cream cheese, softened
¼ cup powdered sugar

½ teaspoon grated orange peel
½ cup sliced fresh strawberries

In small bowl, combine cream cheese, powdered sugar and orange peel; beat until smooth. Add strawberries; beat until well blended. Store in refrigerator.

Yield: 1¼ cups

Nutrition Information Per Serving
Serving Size: 1 Tablespoon. Calories 50 • Calories from Fat 35 • Total Fat 4 g • Saturated Fat 2 g • Cholesterol 10 mg • Sodium 35 mg • Dietary Fiber 0 g
Dietary Exchange: 1 Fat

About Strawberries

Top-quality strawberries make a difference in this recipe. Choose berries that are uniformly red with no white patches. Check the package carefully and avoid any with signs of mold. Rinse, hull and slice the berries immediately before use.

gift idea

Rum and Pecan Cream Cheese Spread

Prep Time: 10 minutes
(Ready in 2 hours 10 minutes)

1 (8-oz.) container cream cheese
¼ cup chopped pecans

¼ teaspoon rum extract
1 to 2 teaspoons milk

In small bowl, combine all ingredients, adding enough milk for desired spreading consistency; blend well. Cover; refrigerate at least 2 hours to blend flavors. Store in refrigerator.

Yield: 1 cup

Nutrition Information Per Serving
Serving Size: 1 Tablespoon. Calories 60 • Calories from Fat 50 • Total Fat 6 g • Saturated Fat 3 g • Cholesterol 15 mg • Sodium 40 mg • Dietary Fiber 0 g
Dietary Exchange: 1 Fat

Recipe Fact

Rum extract and chopped pecans give the spread nice flavor without becoming overly sweet.

Cranberry Spread

1 (3-oz.) pkg. cream cheese,
   softened
½ cup powdered sugar
¼ cup margarine or butter,
   softened

1 teaspoon vanilla
¼ cup chopped fresh or frozen
   cranberries

In small bowl, combine cream cheese, powdered sugar, margarine and vanilla; beat until light and fluffy. Stir in cranberries. Store in refrigerator.

Yield: ¾ cup

Nutrition Information Per Serving

Serving Size: 1 Tablespoon. Calories 80 • Calories from Fat 50 • Total Fat 6 g • Saturated Fat 2 g • Cholesterol 10 mg • Sodium 65 mg • Dietary Fiber 0 g
Dietary Exchanges: ½ Fruit, 1 Fat OR ½ Carbohydrate, 1 Fat

Make It Special

Shape the spread into a log, then refrigerate to firm it up. Before serving, roll the log in minced nuts.

Recipe Variation

Achieve a similarly lovely pink color but different flavor by making the spread with fresh or frozen raspberries or strawberries in place of the cranberries.

Cherry-Almond Cream Cheese Spread

Prep Time: 10 minutes
(Ready in 2 hours 10 minutes)

1 (8-oz.) container cream
   cheese

2 tablespoons cherry preserves
¼ teaspoon almond extract

In small bowl, combine all ingredients; blend well. Cover; refrigerate at least 2 hours to blend flavors. Store in refrigerator.

Yield: 1 cup

Nutrition Information Per Serving

Serving Size: 1 Tablespoon. Calories 60 • Calories from Fat 45 • Total Fat 5 g • Saturated Fat 3 g • Cholesterol 15 mg • Sodium 45 mg • Dietary Fiber 0 g
Dietary Exchange: 1 Fat

editor's favorite   *gift idea*

Kitchen Tip

Soften the cream cheese for about an hour at room temperature to make blending in the preserves easier.

Make It Special

Mound the spread into a decorative serving dish and press toasted almond slivers into the top.

Lemon-Spiced Cream Cheese Spread

Prep Time: 10 minutes
(Ready in 2 hours 10 minutes)

Recipe Variation

Flavor the cream cheese spread with orange peel instead of lemon.

1 (8-oz.) container cream cheese
1 teaspoon sugar
½ teaspoon grated lemon peel

¼ teaspoon cinnamon
⅛ teaspoon cloves
1 to 2 teaspoons milk

In small bowl, combine all ingredients, adding enough milk for desired spreading consistency; blend well. Cover; refrigerate at least 2 hours to blend flavors. Store in refrigerator.

Yield: 1 cup

Nutrition Information Per Serving

Serving Size: 1 Tablespoon. Calories 50 • Calories from Fat 45 • Total Fat 5 g • Saturated Fat 3 g • Cholesterol 15 mg • Sodium 40 mg • Dietary Fiber 0 g
Dietary Exchange: 1 Fat

● low-fat

Creamy Honey Spread

Prep Time: 5 minutes

Make It Special

For a pretty gift, wrap your favorite quick bread in colored plastic wrap and add a festive bow. Include the spread packed in a small crock and sprinkled with grated nutmeg.

1 (8-oz.) pkg. ⅓-less-fat cream cheese (Neufchâtel), softened

2 tablespoons honey
⅛ teaspoon nutmeg

In small bowl, combine all ingredients; beat until smooth. Store in refrigerator.

Yield: 1 cup

Nutrition Information Per Serving

Serving Size: 1 Tablespoon. Calories 35 • Calories from Fat 20 • Total Fat 2 g • Saturated Fat 2 g • Cholesterol 5 mg • Sodium 65 mg • Dietary Fiber 0 g
Dietary Exchange: ½ Fat

Roasted Garlic Spread

gift idea

Prep Time: 15 minutes
(Ready in 1 hour)

14 unpeeled garlic cloves   **½ cup butter, softened**

1. Heat oven to 400°F. Wrap garlic cloves in foil. Bake at 400°F. for 40 minutes or until very soft.
2. Open foil; cool garlic 5 minutes or until cool to the touch.
3. Slip garlic cloves from skins into small bowl; discard skins. Mash cloves with fork. Beat in butter until light and fluffy. Store in refrigerator for up to 2 weeks.

Yield: ½ cup

Nutrition Information Per Serving

Serving Size: 1 Tablespoon. Calories 120 • Calories from Fat 110 • Total Fat 12 g • Saturated Fat 7 g • Cholesterol 30 mg • Sodium 120 mg • Dietary Fiber 0 g
Dietary Exchange: 2½ Fat

Kitchen Tip

Garlic loses its sharp edge as it roasts in its skin, taking on a pungent, mellow flavor. The roasted garlic can also be stirred into soups, mashed potatoes or pureed butternut squash.

Make It Special

The garlic spread is great on savory muffins as well as baked potatoes, vegetables and even steak. To serve it attractively, mound it while still soft into a ramekin or similar small dish and sprinkle the top with minced fresh parsley or another favorite herb.

Storage Tip

Make sure to wrap the spread tightly so the butter doesn't absorb refrigerator odors and the garlic's fragrance doesn't permeate other foods.

Index

Conversion Chart
Equivalent Imperial and Metric Measurements

American cooks use standard containers, the 8-ounce cup and a tablespoon that takes exactly 16 level fillings to fill that cup level. Measuring by cup makes it very difficult to give weight equivalents, as a cup of densely packed butter will weigh considerably more than a cup of flour. The easiest way therefore to deal with cup measurements in recipes is to take the amount by volume rather than by weight. Thus the equation reads:

1 cup = 240 ml = 8 fl. oz.   ½ cup = 120 ml = 4 fl. oz.

It is possible to buy a set of American cup measures in major stores around the world.

In the States, butter is often measured in sticks. One stick is the equivalent of 8 tablespoons. One tablespoon of butter is therefore the equivalent to ½ ounce/15 grams.

Solid Measures

U.S. and Imperial Measures		Metric Measures	
Ounces	Pounds	Grams	Kilos
1		28	
2		56	
3½		100	
4	¼	112	
5		140	
6		168	
8	½	225	
9		250	¼
12	¾	340	
16	1	450	
18		500	½
20	1¼	560	
24	1½	675	
27		750	¾
28	1¾	780	
32	2	900	
36	2¼	1000	1
40	2½	1100	
48	3	1350	
54		1500	1½

Liquid Measures

Fluid Ounces	U.S.	Imperial	Milliliters
	1 teaspoon	1 teaspoon	5
¼	2 teaspoons	1 dessertspoon	10
½	1 tablespoon	1 tablespoon	14
1	2 tablespoons	2 tablespoons	28
2	¼ cup	4 tablespoons	56
4	½ cup		110
5		¼ pint or 1 gill	140
6	¾ cup		170
8	1 cup		225
9			250, ¼ liter
10	1¼ cups	½ pint	280
12	1½ cups		340
15		¾ pint	420
16	2 cups		450
18	2¼ cups		500, ½ liter
20	2½ cups	1 pint	560
24	3 cups		675
25		1¼ pints	700
27	3½ cups		750
30	3¾ cups	1½ pints	840
32	4 cups or 1 quart		900
35		1¾ pints	980
36	4½ cups		1000, 1 liter
40	5 cups	2 pints or 1 quart	1120

Oven Temperature Equivalents

Fahrenheit	Celsius	Gas Mark	Description
225	110	¼	Cool
250	130	½	
275	140	1	Very Slow
300	150	2	
325	170	3	Slow
350	180	4	Moderate
375	190	5	
400	200	6	Moderately Hot
425	220	7	Fairly Hot
450	230	8	Hot
475	240	9	Very Hot
500	250	10	Extremely Hot

Any broiling recipes can be used with the grill of the oven, but beware of high-temperature grills.

Equivalents for Ingredients

all-purpose flour—plain flour
coarse salt—kitchen salt
cornstarch—cornflour
eggplant—aubergine

half and half—12% fat milk
heavy cream—double cream
light cream—single cream
lima beans—broad beans

scallion—spring onion
unbleached flour—strong, white flour
zest—rind
zucchini—courgettes or marrow